T0341604

EASY
EGO STATE
INTERVENTIONS

A Norton Professional Book

EASY EGO STATE INTERVENTIONS

Strategies for Working With Parts

ROBIN SHAPIRO

W. W. NORTON & COMPANY
New York · London

Note to Readers: Standards of clinical practice and protocol change over time, and no technique or recommendation is guaranteed to be safe or effective in all circumstances. This volume is intended as a general information resource for professionals practicing in the field of psychotherapy and mental health; it is not a substitute for appropriate training, peer review, and/or clinical supervision. Neither the publisher nor the author(s) can guarantee the complete accuracy, efficacy, or appropriateness of any particular recommendation in every respect.

Copyright © 2016 by Robin Shapiro

All rights reserved
Printed in the United States of America
First Edition

For information about permission to reproduce selections from this book, write to Permissions, W. W. Norton & Company, Inc., 500 Fifth Avenue, New York, NY 10110

For information about special discounts for bulk purchases, please contact W. W. Norton Special Sales at specialsales@wwnorton.com or 800-233-4830

Manufacturing by Sheridan Books
Book design by Carole Desnoes
Production manager: Christine Critelli

Library of Congress Cataloging-in-Publication Data

Names: Shapiro,
Robin, author.
Title: Easy ego state interventions : strategies for working with parts /
Robin Shapiro.
Description: First edition. | New York : W.W. Norton & Company, [2016] | Series:
A Norton professional book | Includes bibliographical references and index.
Identifiers: LCCN
2015036836 | ISBN 9780393709278 (hardcover)
Subjects: LCSH: Dissociative disorders. | Dissociation (Psychology) |
Ego (Psychology) | Psychotherapy.
Classification: LCC RC553.D5 S53 2016 | DDC
616.85/23--dc23
LC record available at http://lccn.loc.gov/2015036836

W. W. Norton & Company, Inc.
500 Fifth Avenue, New York, N.Y. 10110
www.wwnorton.com

W. W. Norton & Company Ltd.
15 Carlisle Street, London W1D 3BS

To David Calof, April Steele,
and all the teachers, clinicians, and clients
who have taught me about "parts."

CONTENTS

ACKNOWLEDGMENTS

Thank you to the people who supported this book:

Andrea Costella, at Norton, who let me talk her into talking the committee into publishing this book and then improved it with her insightful edit, and Benjamin Yarling, my new editor. Trish Watson, the copy editor, and all the folks at Norton, for seeing it through to publishing.

David Calof, who has supported me through most of my career with good advice and most of what I know about parts, states, and clinical hypnosis. And the members of our long-running consultation group, Helen Estoque and Doug McLemore.

Kathy Steele, Onno van der Hart, and Ellert Nijenhuis for giving the therapy world a simple and elegant way to make sense of ego states, one of the organizing principles of this work. And Kathy Steele, again, for giving me the right words to explain structural dissociation.

Hemda Arad, for her time, knowledge, and expertise in all things psychodynamic for this book and the last.

All the clinicians, trainers, and writers who laid the basis for my understanding of this work: Jim Knipe, Thom Negri, Carol Forgash, Sandra Paulsen, Eric Berne, Peggy Pace, Joanne Twombly, and many more.

The clients who freely gave their stories and who were and are the collaborators in every ego state intervention.

Elinor Welt, my first reader and first editor for all four books, who tightened the language, made me add "2 percent more" for clarity, and chased down every missing comma. Thanks, Mom!

Doug Plummer, my wonderful husband, who didn't even sigh when I told him that I felt another book coming on.

ACRONYMS AND ABBREVIATIONS

ANP	apparently normal part
CIMBS	complex integration of multiple brain systems
DID	dissociative identity disorder, formerly multiple personality diagnosis
EMDR	eye movement desensitization and reprocessing
EP	emotional part
PTSD	posttraumatic stress disorder

EASY
EGO STATE
INTERVENTIONS

INTRODUCTION

If you are new to ego state therapy, welcome to a powerful, flexible therapy. If you are an old hand, I hope you find some new interventions to add to your therapeutic toolbox.

Before we delve into the how-tos and whys of ego state therapy, let me give you an example of a general ego state intervention, helpful to a variety of people, especially therapists. If you want to experience it yourself, shut your eyes occasionally in order to access your own particular "states."

Go inside. Notice, as you sit deeply into your chair, that you are an adult. As an adult, you have boundaries. You have professional and other skills. And you have a broad perspective. Think of yourself acting competently with clients, paying bills, voting, and behaving as an adult in your relationships . . . Now go deeper, and as that competent adult, find that small child inside of you. Notice how that child holds your curiosity, your need to elicit love and approval, and for many of you, because you chose this profession, the need to take care of those around you.

When you've found that little one inside, look at it and feel its gaze coming back to you and let yourself know if this little one inside deserves to be taken care of: fed, protected, allowed normal sleep, loved, kept around loving people and everything else a human needs. Will you commit to taking care of this child in you? . . . And will you, as an adult, keep this child back from situations in which you need to be and act like an adult? . . . Good. Now I want you to imagine walking through a normal day attending to adult things, while taking care of and protecting this child. Make sure this child is fed, hydrated, well slept, and entertained. Make sure that your adult self keeps this child out of situations that call for adult behavior. Walk through letting your adult decide what your boundaries will be with your work, your families, and the needs of all others . . . When you're ready, hug that child inside, feel that young heart beating inside your heart and those little lungs breathing with you, and come back, fully to the room and this book.

What did we just do?

- III   We changed your "state" by closing your eyes and going "inside."
- III   We accessed the adult functional part of you, including an adult role.
- III   We accessed a child state and normalized some of its functions.
- III   We connected the two states.
- III   We put the adult state in charge and got its agreement that the child state is its responsibility. Then we delineated those responsibilities.

▌▌▌ For some of you, we gave a new way to think about self-
care and boundaries.

▌▌▌ And at the end, we integrated the younger part back inside
the here-and-now adult.

I learned parts of this exercise in the early 1980s from Thom
Negri (personal communication, 1981). At that time, I had a
passing acquaintance with Sigmund Freud's id, ego, and super-
ego (Freud, 1933, pp. 105–106) and had read about Eric Berne's
(1964) transactional analysis and its famous three circles (P for
parent, A for adult, and C for child). Later I learned the gestalt
"two-chair" technique and studied deeply with hypnotherapists,
especially David Calof ("go inside"), who often called up ego
states for therapeutic effect. In the mid-1980s, I started working with my first dissociative identity disorder (DID) client. As
I quickly learned, anyone working effectively with DID must
respond to ego states. In 1993, I learned eye movement desensitization and reprocessing (EMDR), the powerful trauma therapy,
which at the time did not address dissociation. Because there
is no faster way to awaken dissociative phenomena than to do
EMDR without proper preparation, there are now at least eleven
books and countless workshops (some of which I have taught)
dealing directly with EMDR and dissociation, most of which
discuss ego state work. Joanne Twombly and Richard Schwartz's
"The Integration of the Internal Family Systems Model (IFS)
and EMDR" (2008) introduced me to the comprehensive internal family systems model. Workshops and online forums at the
International Society for Study of Trauma and Dissociation gave
me many other tools for working with dissociative individuals.

In this book I want to share the interventions that have worked for my clients that you may not have seen elsewhere. I hope this book is helpful to therapists new to ego state work and to veterans of the modality wanting new interventions to add to their toolbox.

Ego state therapy works well with every other therapy that I know about: explore inappropriate cognitions with examinations of which ages hold them; enhance the safe, present-moment strong adult before exposure to the traumatized younger parts; expand on the built-in ego states in psychodynamic therapies; make it possible to do EMDR with the most traumatized and dissociated clients by having the functional parts hold and behold the traumatized ones; find the "brainspot" that fits with the age or dissociated part (Grand, 2013). And, if you have simple trauma, or a client who simply needs some new skills, you might not need ego state therapy at all.

Many of the interventions in *Easy Ego State Interventions* are as universal as the example I gave above, suitable for "garden-variety" clients with normal developmental issues, such as differentiation from families and peer groups, self-care, and grief. Many of the interventions will also work with clients across the dissociation spectrum, a condition particularly well suited to ego state work, including clients who suffer trauma and complex trauma. This book offers ego state approaches that work for both client populations, though a thorough discussion of dissociation is beyond the scope of this book.

Be aware that when clinicians talk about ego state therapy they are often talking about dissociative state therapy, not ego state work with garden-variety clients. Are they talking about here-and-now, associated, but sometimes younger-feeling parts of the self ("garden variety" ego state work), or reflexively triggered, dissociated, separate parts? I discuss both throughout this book.

While I discuss dissociation in Chapter 1, *Easy Ego State Interventions* will not teach you all you need to know about dissociation. For that, I suggest *Ego States: Theory and Therapy* (Watkins & Watkins, 1997), *The Haunted Self* (van der Hart, Nijenhuis, & Steele, 2006), and *Coping With Trauma-Related Dissociation* (Boon & Steele, 2011) For EMDR practitioners, *Healing the Heart of Trauma and Dissociation* (Forgash & Copely, 2007), *EMDR Toolbox: Theory and Treatment of Complex PTSD and Dissociation* (Knipe, 2014), and *Neurobiology and Treatment of Traumatic Dissociation: Towards an Embodied Self* (Lanius & Paulsen, 2014).

If you have never done ego state work with clients, it may feel odd to ask, *how old does that feel?* or, *what part of you holds that thought?* Most clients pause for a moment and answer the question. Some clients, after a session or two of "going inside," start giving reports: "My obnoxious teenager came out at a party this weekend." "My geeky ten-year-old really loved the science museum." "I really had to work hard to stay in my adult when I went to that job interview, but I nailed it."

Other clients need more help to understand your questions. I work to find the metaphors about ego states that fit individual clients. In techy Seattle, I often tell clients about *old internal programs that need an upgrade, in order to connect to the newest operating system and data. In fact that's how you can conceptualize your whole therapy.* Other clients grasp more organic explanations:

For every age and learning situation, we develop neural pathways. We've got them for right now, and all our current experiences, and we have them for every age and everything we've learned. Sometimes old pathways arise, and we feel and do things that belong to the past, when the more current ones might work better. This work gives us a way to connect the "right now" parts of our brains with the "back then" parts so that you are feeling and doing what's right for "now."

Some clients need no explanation. Ask them to "go inside" and find the age that the feeling belongs to, and they go right there, the first time. Some clients, often but not always the most dissociative, resist strongly. "I don't want to do that inner child stuff! I don't have one!" "Robin, that's woo-woo bullshit!" Van der Hart et al. (2006) in their theory of structural dissociation call this a phobia of their trauma or their parts. My usual response is to switch from asking about "parts" to asking about "states": *We don't have to do that right now. When you think about doing that kind of work, what are you feeling inside?* (Notice I don't ask, *What is your objection?* That question would keep the client in thought. I want them feeling and talking about it.) Answers might range from fear to anger (with fear underneath). One person told me that she had previously been diagnosed with DID and didn't want to deal with those parts again. ("Gee, thanks for telling me," I didn't say out loud.) Most have built big defenses against feeling old, overwhelming emotions. We explore that, referring to the steps of working with structural dissociation: *Before we touch any of the old stuff, we're going to build up your here-and-now adult. When we do deal with the old trauma and old programming, we're going to do it in small pieces and keep you right here, right now, knowing that you're safe, while we do it.*

Once in a great while, you might start with a basic ego state question, *can you go inside and find the age that goes with that fear?*, and find that your client has "switched," doesn't know you, and doesn't know where he is. Don't panic—take a deep breath, introduce yourself, what you do, and where you both are. If the client looks terrified, let him know that you never hurt anyone.

Ask a few questions about his age, his name (it could be different than your client's presenting name), and his circumstances. Let that dissociated part of your client know that you would like to talk to him again. Then say, *You can sleep now, and I want to talk to the part of* (client's name) *that first walked into the office.*

This has surprised me twice in my career, and I have heard from many consultees, sometime in frantic in-session phone calls, who have had the same experience. It helps to have done screening for dissociation at the intake, but it doesn't catch everyone. When you have made sure that your client is all there in his most adult self and knows his children's names and his workplace, you can let him go home. Then you can take a class from the International Society for the Study of Trauma and Dissociation, start reading books about dissociation, and join a new consultation group.

I use italics throughout the book to mark what a therapist says to a client. Sometimes I teach by showing, not by explaining, and the italics will show you what you might say to your clients. Of course, you will modify everything you say to fit your style and the needs of the client in front of you.

Chapter 1, which defines and contextualizes ego state work, will have the most technical material. The chapters that follow discuss specific interventions for specific problems, with many case examples. These examples, although derived from actual cases in my practice, are composites—they do not represent transcripts of actual sessions, and use fictitious names. They nonetheless exemplify approaches and dialogue I have found effective in my practice.

I hope this book will give you new ways to see your clients and new therapeutic skills. I wish you good work, and your clients good healing.

EASY
EGO STATE
INTERVENTIONS

Part I

GETTING STARTED WITH EGO STATE WORK

CHAPTER 1

Defining and Diagnosing Ego States

Ego states are bundles of neural connections that hold consistent patterns of information, affect, attention, behavior, and sometimes identity, which belong to specific developmental ages or situations.

Humans, like other animals, have wiring for all kinds of states. We are wired for waking, sleeping, eating, connecting, playing, showing aggression, curiosity, and, when needed, inhibiting those states. Jaak Panksepp (1998) shows that the neural wiring of a playful rat and a playful human stimulate similar, preprogrammed areas of the brain. Daniel Hughes and Jonathan Baylin (2012) explain that infants can develop different neural networks of connection and expectation for the different caregivers in their life. For example, a child might be in a calm, connected state for her calm, nurturing mom; an excited, happy state for her playful, rough-housing dad; and an agitated, distressed state around her abusive big brother. Research shows that the child may move into those states on encountering the person, before a new interaction.

The neurons in our big brains are constantly preparing us for the future. We have organized neuronal clusters that habitually do, feel, and think, mostly in an unconscious, automatic way. When we have a new experience, do new activities, go to a new place, or feel a strong feeling, our brains start to build connections with the thoughts, emotions, and actions that go with the new experience. If life or conscious practice puts us in the same situation over and over, we develop thousands of thicker, stronger neuronal connections. We have conscious and unconscious programs for most of what we do and much of what we think and feel. Imagine what it would be like if you had to think about every action that goes with driving a car, making coffee, taking a shower, or talking with a friend. While some of us strive for a meditative "beginners mind," imagine the hassles if we actually had one! Every tiny action we take would have to be thoroughly thought through. Babies and other people in the "first time ever doing this" situation are the only people who do and feel and figure things out without using these internal templates. Even then, internal programs are at work.

Therapists rarely need to discuss action systems for daily reactions, activities, and the thousands of habitual modes, preferences, and reflexive opinions that clients have in their lives. Most clients can walk, talk, and read and get through most of their life activities without therapeutic intervention. But when regular states become compromised by distressing situations, illness, lack of appropriate response from caretakers, a panic attack, a severe traumatic event, or chronic developmental abuse, neuronal connections can solidify into rigid dysfunctional ego states that pop up to impede optimal current-day functioning.

On the more severe end of the spectrum, traumatized or affectively overwhelmed clients may shut down one set of neural responses and start a new set going. Their regulated states may be compromised. Babies, when overstimulated in a positive way, may turn away and blank out for a moment, to reset their nervous system. When highly distressed, they may go from neutral to a completely agitated/mobilized state to a completely slack/immobilized state in minutes (Tronick, Adamson, Als, & Brazelton, 1975). Most humans, in the experience of overwhelming trauma, will create a neural imprint of that traumatic experience, sometimes going to a "mobilized" fight-or-flight state and other times to an "immobilized," slack, giving-up state (Porges, 2011). If the trauma is intense enough or repetitive, the ego state may become a dissociative state, disconnected to the present time while holding the behaviors, thoughts, and feelings tied to past situations and past identities.

WHY EGO STATE WORK?

Ego state interventions bring appropriate chosen (not reflexive) capacities to current functioning. Ego state work can

III   create awareness of normal or pathological state switching and bring it under conscious control;

III   bring a mature adult state to the front to deal with people, situations, and emotions;

III   heal trauma by creating a true "dual attention" between parts stuck in a traumatic event and the here-and-now

adult in the relatively safe world, and then pull the traumatized part into the safe present in an integrative way;

III   bring former resources to current situations (*Can you get
in touch with the playful kid inside of you? How would he
approach this situation?* Or, *Think of a time when you were in
control of your life. What did that feel like? Can you bring that
piece of you up to this time?*);

III   with more dissociated clients, bring the adult apparently
normal parts (ANPs) into conscious stewardship of all
states (Van der Hart et al., 2006);

III   perform parentectomies, removing negative parental introjects;

III   perform abusectomies, removing lingering sensations and
thoughts of abuse; and perform culturectomies, removing
internalized cultural strictures (think expectations about
race, appearance, class, gender roles, etc.).

UNDERSTANDING RESOURCED EGO STATES

When doing ego state work, therapists tend to focus on two
states: positive resourced ego states and dysfunctional, reactive,
not-connected-to-present-reality states.

Resourced states can be the grown-up, capable ego states
and, if dissociative, ANPs "Apparently Normal Parts" (van der
Hart et al., 2006) that take care of the business of daily life,
know where and when they are, and have thoughts and emotions appropriate for what is going on around them. If a client
feels unable to cope, a therapist might ask her to think about a
moment of triumph, to recall the thoughts and emotions that
went with it, and to bring these thoughts, feelings, and capac-

ities to the new situation (Leeds, 2009). A therapist may call on a client's internal scientist to examine his family dynamics from a detached and curious point of view. *Imagine that you're an anthropologist, researching the mores of people at your family reunion. What would you see there?* Or call up the "oldest/wisest" part of self that can handle a situation better than a reflexively present child part: *Can you bring up that grown-up oldest, wisest part of you to handle that interview? I think she might do it better than this scared kid part of you, who is anticipating not being wanted.*

Sometimes the resources come from outside the client, but not outside his experience. Therapists who call for imagined protectors, nurturers, or spiritual figures (Parnell, 2013; Schmidt, 2009) are using external resources. Resourced states can be

III adult parts: parental, professional, sexual, intellectual parts based in the present;

III nurturing parts: choicefully able to take care of self and others, in the best cases, modeled on the nurturing received from others, and in other cases constructed from imagined nurturing;

III protective parts: boundary setting, assertive, skilled with conflict, knowing when to run, and when and how to fight;

III spiritual core/the self/the core: often carries core identity, connection with spirituality/the planet/God, the part that has always been and will always be; and

III parts with particular skills needed for current functioning: technical skills, specific knowledge.

UNDERSTANDING DYSFUNCTIONAL EGO STATES

Dysfunctional states are bundled thoughts, emotions, and reactions that are inappropriate for the current time. Think of arguments you have had with your significant other. Did you manage to stay in your most rational and adult self through every argument? Probably not! When you were not in "adult" mode, you were likely in a not-so-functional ego state, based on other interactions with your family of origin, spouse, or past relationships. Wouldn't it have been great if your calm, compassionate, mature adult self had been in charge of your emotions, words, and actions during every conflict?

Distressing events, especially events that feel physically ("I'm going to die!") or socially ("You'll leave me!") dangerous, can create strong neuronal clusters, that can be triggered in current circumstances.

Types of dysfunctional ego states

- Parts or states that are not in line with adaptive behavior, emotions, and conceptions about present circumstances; may be dissociative, affective, or merely habitual
- Mobilized, protective states (Porges, 2011):
  - Hyperalert
  - Terrified and ready to run
  - Angry and ready to fight
  - Distinguished from protective "resource" states by being inappropriate for current circumstances
- Immobilized states (Porges, 2011):
  - Hopeless/helpless

   I   Inert/depressed
   I   Shame filled
III   Introjects, modeled on the dysfunctional behavior of care-
       givers or abusers

All of these dysfunctional states manifest as behaviors and feelings better suited to surviving in the past than in the present.

Nondissociative Dysfunctional Ego States

In the 1980s, when the traffic helicopters flew overhead, my clients who were Vietnam veterans would shift into an alert stance,
become very directive (or aggressive), and shut down any emotional processing. I learned to say, *Stand down, soldier, and tell me
what just happened*, in order to have them shift from the func-
tional-but-not-for-now states they would be triggered into. They
became able to notice when the "soldier" popped up in current
life and when they needed to orient to the present time. The
patterns in the "soldier" were helpful at times of emergencies
but did not work very well in child-rearing, in conflict resolution
at home or at work, or in dealing with their own or anyone else's
emotions. The veterans learned to orient themselves to the present and identify "the right man for the job" in a conscious way.

Most often, therapists work with child states that pop up in
adult situations. For instance, clients with social anxiety will
often default to their "scared kid" states, when approaching a
new situation. I ask,

> *How old is that kid that's terrified to go to that meeting?*
> Thirteen.

What does your adult know that that kid doesn't?
I know that people like me, that I know what I'm doing and
how to present myself.

Which part of you is better equipped to be at that meeting?
The adult!

So which part of you are you sending to the meeting?
I know. I'm sending my grown-up and remembering that I
am one.

What happens to the kid part?
I'm letting her know that I'm handling it and that she can
settle down.

Understanding Introjects

When we are lucky, we carry the nurturing and good examples
of our caregivers and role models around inside of us—these are
positive introjects. Well-attached, well-nurtured children will
sooth themselves with the hugs and comforting words that came
from their parents: "It's okay. You'll be all right." These children
contain sweet self-states that mirror their sweet parents' advice,
cautions, and positive affect. As the children grow, they absorb
concepts, behavior, affect, and even mannerisms from other kids,
teachers, and whoever is around.

We carry the bad stuff, too. Sensitive children can absorb
their parents' anxiety, rage, or depression. Battered children can
replicate their abusive parents' voices and threats. Sexually abused
children learn, "This is what I'm for." "I don't exist for myself."

"I'm damaged goods." Sometimes they learn, "This is what you do to other kids." All of these children can develop states that mimic the parents' abuse or demeanor. With consistent abuse, neglect, or lack of positive mirroring, kids can develop an interior voice that criticizes them for any behavior that may bring negative consequences from a caregiver. Sometimes these voices are meaner than the actual parent.

Understanding Dissociative Ego States

The above examples of ego states may be dysfunctional, but they are not necessarily dissociative. What's the difference? Many ego states arise from job descriptions: the part of me that knows how to do therapy; the part of me that knows how to relate to cats; my nurturer; my aggressive competitor; and so forth. Dissociation arises from a person's reflexive attempt to deal with attachment ruptures or trauma by shifting into a separate neural gear, disconnected from the core self. Dissociative "parts" are more strongly delineated, because survival was at stake when they arose.

Edward Tronick posted a video of the still face experiment (Tronick, 2007), findable on the Web, in which a happy, healthy baby, with a good mom, goes from "reaching out" to "distress" to "anger" to "shut down" in a matter of minutes when the mom stops responding. Kids with longer, unrepaired ruptures of attachment reflexively dissociate when they are not responded to (Putnam, 1997). A child with a nonresponsive, substance-abusing, depressed, anxious, or overburdened caregiver can grow entrenched dissociative patterns in attachment disorders that may manifest as borderline or schizoid personality disorder. Kids with scary, unpredictable (also scary), or abusive parents may develop a dissociative part to deal with each state of their care-givers.

Kathy Steele, the brilliant clinician, trainer, and writer, told me:

Ego states have permeable boundaries, unlike many dissocia-tive parts. They do not involve amnesia; that is, one ego state is not operating in the outside world without the awareness of another ego state. Ego states do not create "jarring" intrusions into the experience of the person as do dissociative parts. Ego states do not cause a person to experience first-ranked Schnei-derian symptoms of schizophrenia: hearing voices comment-ing or arguing, feeling your body is controlled by someone else; made thoughts, feelings, or impulses, and so on. They do not have a separate sense of self as dissociative parts do. Ego states experience themselves as the person, albeit perhaps in a different state or age or time.

Dissociative *responses* may include "spacing out," a reflex-ive opioid response to a distressing emotion or situation, espe-cially in the case of early trauma or attachment disruption (Schore, 2001). They may be affective states, such as anger, deep shame, or fear, tied to another time.

Dissociative *ego states* are more complex. They

  | often have their own identities and sense of self;
  | have a characteristic self-representation, which may not be consistent with the self-representation of the individ-ual as whole;
  | have their own set of autobiographical memories, which may be different than other dissociative parts;
  | may have a sense of ownership of their own thoughts,

feelings, actions, and so on—a good rule to follow: "all dissociative parts are ego states, but not all ego states are dissociative parts" (K. Steele, personal communication, September 19, 2009; via Shapiro, 2010).

ASSESSING DISSOCIATION

When a newish client, beginning to have a strong emotion, suddenly looks curiously around the room and says in a childish voice, "Where is this? Who are you?" it is easy to see the dissociation (and probable DID diagnosis). This client obviously has amnesia between parts and will switch when triggered. Most dissociative clients are more adaptive and better at keeping a veneer of a presenting personality while switching inside. A client who shows several of the following has dissociation:

||| Spaces out easily
||| Loses coherence when speaking about childhood events (Siegel, 1999)
||| Can't remember much of childhood years
||| Begins to use different voices, inflections, or age-specific language
||| Abruptly switches from calm discussion to a hostile, terrified, shut-down, or disorganized state
||| Is easily triggered into feelings of abandonment, defensiveness, or clinginess
||| Subtly or not so subtly changes stance and expression in a "weird" way
||| Has otherwise unexplained headaches, nausea, or pelvic pain

ııı   Does not connect with you
ııı   Shows inappropriate affect when discussing distressing
      events
ııı   Speaks in the third person about the self
ııı   Forgets appointments, despite a good therapeutic relationship

The theory of structural dissociation by van der Hart et al.
(2006) describes three levels of dissociation:

1.   Primary dissociation or posttraumatic stress disorder
     (PTSD), when the here-and-now "apparently normal part"
     (ANP) experiences the PTSD "emotional part" (EP) night-
     mares, startle response, flashbacks, and hypervigilance as an
     intrusion on normal life
2.   Secondary dissociation (personality disorders), in which the
     ANP can shift into habitual childish EP states that might
     be raging or clingy (borderline), shame filled versus defen-
     sive (narcissistic), or "I don't need anyone, I'm okay, and I'm
     not feeling anything" schizoid states
3.   Tertiary dissociation, or DID, in which there are at least
     two ANPs taking care of business and often several EPs
     that hold different experiences, emotions, and functions and
     have little knowledge of each other.

One more category, not specifically mentioned by van der Hart et
al. (2006), is people who were or are abused in organized settings
through ritual abuse or mind control. These people are usually
fragmented into many amnestic pieces and need specialized treatment for management of their parts and, often, their safety.

Because few clients announce that they have secondary dissociation (personality, character, or Axis II disorders) or tertiary dissociation (DID or dissociative disorders, not otherwise specified), clinicians often use diagnostic tools to screen every client for dissociative disorders, some of which I list below. Make sure you get much more information than I give you in this book. If you know that you are working with highly dissociative clients, please make sure you read the books, go to the workshops, and attend good consultation in order to give them the best therapy you can.

Tools for screening for dissociation

||| The Dissociative Experiences Scale is a twenty-eight-item questionnaire in which the client reports on the prevalence of common and not-so-common dissociative experiences. It is easily rated for degrees of dissociation from PTSD to DID (Bernstein & Putnam, 1986).

||| The Dissociative Disorders Interview Schedule is a comprehensive 132-item highly structured interview. It evaluates depression, borderline personality disorder, and all levels of dissociation. Download it for free from Dr. Colin Ross, its creator, at http://www.rossinst.com/ddis.html (see also Ross, 1997). Just by reading it you will become a better diagnostician.

||| The Somatoform Questionnaire, available in twenty-item and five-item versions, evaluates somatoform dissociation (physical and sensory experiences) and other dissociative disorders. It is available from Ellert Nijenhuis's website at http://www.enijenhuis.nl/index.html.

In the remaining chapters in Part I of the book, I discuss

foundational interventions used for most ego state work. In Part II, I lead you through specific interventions for very specific kinds of clients and issues, including working with traumatized clients, relationship and attachment issues, personality disorders, suicidal ideation, and cultural, familial, and abuse-related introjects.

This section adapted from The Trauma Treatment Handbook by Robin Shapiro, published by W.W. Norton.

CHAPTER 2

Foundational Intervention: Accessing Positive States

For me, the point of therapy is for our clients to become happy, functional, and relatable people. The point of ego state therapy is to find internal resources, bring them to the front of consciousness, enhance them, have them help heal the distressed parts, and bring choice and conscious control to the whole of each client's system. Clients often enter therapy with their mobilized states (anxiety and anger) or immobilized states (depression, hopelessness, helplessness; Porges, 2011) running the show. These states need to be connected with and cared for by their most current, functional states, or ANPs (van der Hart et al., 2006). What do these ANPs do?

||| Protect: keeping safe and holding the awareness/feeling of current safety
||| Hold the abilities and information for daily functioning
||| Nurture self or others

||| Connect to parts of self or others

||| Hold information: the part that holds the

  | hope,

  | awareness that abuse or neglect wasn't the client's fault,

  | compassion for self and others,

  | anger at abuse or neglect that happened to the client,

  | knowledge that it gets better,

  | data on running a grown-up life, and

  | a broader perspective, possibly including

    – a spiritual view,

    – the "big picture,

    – a sense of the whole world, and

    – a sense of connection to others

Accessing and then fostering these normal, positive states within clients is at the heart of ego state therapy. Before any issue-specific work can be done—for example, relationship problems, depression, substance abuse, or trauma—it is important to understand how to elicit these positive states in your clients.

CREATING POSITIVE, FUNCTIONAL EGO STATES

Every effective therapy finds a way for clients to switch into and stay in the appropriate "gear" for the long, connectable, workable haul. In ego state therapy, we can go directly to the positive state. You often start by calling out an adult role, those already thick neural networks of function, information, and identity: the adult, familiar roles, and specific skills and feeling states.

The "Adult"

The most common intervention is to assume a functional adult position and ask for that part to appear:

||| *Can you bring the oldest-wisest part of you forward?*
||| *Are you in your full adult?*
||| *What age is having this reaction? It's your five-year-old? Can you connect to your most adult part? What's your adult reaction? What does your adult think about this?* Jim Knipe asks that the adult part look at the child with "loving eyes," and ask, "When you look at that child, can you see the child's feelings?" (2014, p. 176).

Familiar Roles

Ask your clients to assume one of their familiar roles:

||| *Let me talk to the good parent part of you. How does he see the situation?*
||| *Where's that smart attorney? Bring her in for a consult on this. What feels different, now that she's here?*
||| *Bring up your chef, the one that can be pulling together fifteen meals, dealing with the vendors, and all the staff, while directing traffic in that huge kitchen. Could he set a limit with your mom?*

Specific Adult Skills and Feeling States

Other techniques for accessing positive ego states include

⊩ Finding the adult: *Think about a time when you felt in charge, were in charge, and were taking care of business. Tell me about it. What does that feel like? Where do you feel that in your body? What thoughts go with that?* (adapted from Leeds, 2009)

⊩ Finding specific skills: *What part of you knows how to deal with that? Let's get that piece of you front and center!*

⊩ Finding specific feeling states: *Can you remember when you had a different feeling in that situation? Is there another feeling in the room when you're connecting with me, right here and right now?* (Sheldon & Sheldon, 2010)

ENHANCING FUNCTIONAL EGO STATES

Sometimes ANPs are functional but are stuck in emotions and beliefs about the world that arose during their creation. Here are some common not-so-helpful beliefs that these functional parts can hold:

⊩ "The world is dangerous and I have to be on red alert every minute. So
  ⎮ I can't trust anyone.
  ⎮ I have to do it all myself.
  ⎮ I can't get close to anyone.
  ⎮ being calm is being unsafe."
⊩ "I have to do everything all by myself, with no help, because
  ⎮ no one else is competent" (true in some childhoods).
  ⎮ it's not okay to ask for help."
  ⎮ that's the way I've always done it."

III | people will see I'm doing it wrong."
III "If I notice any other parts of me, I'll be overwhelmed or it means I'm crazy."
III "Other parts are not really me/bad."
III "I can never take a break. I must work 24/7 or
I everything will fall apart.
I I'm not good enough.
I I'll feel the bad stuff that's inside."
III I'm not really competent. I've got them all fooled.

INVENTING NEW POSITIVE FUNCTIONAL STATES

Some people have little experience of being functional or of positive feelings, especially a positive sense of self. For these clients, it is necessary to "build in" the experience of competent function. I often use this with highly dissociative clients, but it can work with garden-variety ego states.

Future Functional Self

III Know what your client needs:
I An adult self to navigate a particular situation
I A part that is not mired in past trauma
I A part that can contain and nurture other parts
I All of the above, or more
III Imagine it: *Imagine your older, wiser self five years from now when you're done with therapy and leading your full life without trauma, with a clear footing in that future time and all the skills you need to take care of yourself, inside and outside.*

    | *What does your body feel when you're in touch with that part?*

    | *What can you say about yourself when you're connected with the larger perspective that your future self has?*

    | *What can you do differently when you're feeling that future self?*

    | *How can she help you in your current situation?*

||| Practice it: *Imagine calling on this part of you when you're dealing with this current problem. How was that different?*

||| Reinforce it: *Think of all the times in a day that you can call on this part of you for advice, course correction, and support.*

||| Refer to it in therapy:

    | *What's the older, wiser perspective on what's happening?*

    | *Can the older, wiser part*

      – *nurture that kid?*

      – *look at that kid through loving eyes?*

      – *give us his perspective on this situation?*

      – *help us think through what happened?*

      – *tell you how she'd handle the situation?*

||| Find some alternative thoughts and experiences for "there's only danger":

    | *Look around this room. Is it safe right here and right now?*

    | *Where in that older, wiser self is the feeling of safety?*

    | *How does he have that?*

    | *Can she share that with other parts?*

    | *How can you manifest that in your current life?*

    | *How about when a younger part gets scared?* (for dissociative people).

    | *Does that older, wiser self know that you don't have to do everything by yourself, and that there are some people you can rely on?*

III   Find some alternative thoughts and experiences for "I have
to do everything by myself":

I   *Can this part look back to times he has been helped?*

I   *Has she been choosing to be around helpful/loving people?*

I   (If it's unimaginable): *Think of helpful people you've heard
about. Parts of you may hold too much defense or shame to
connect with your experience or memory of any helpful connections. I want you to think ahead to twenty years from now,
when you will have had some better experiences. You may even
think of this therapy as helpful. Can that part of you from
twenty years from now inform the rest of you what it was like
to be helped and to know that you're not alone? Can he connect
to all of you and let you know that you can accept help?*

Developing and Using a Conference Room of Resources for Client Stabilization

Here is Roy Kiessling's (2005) elegant (and fun) mechanism that
introduces and solidifies attributes for clients' adult parts:

III   Identify what the needs of the moment are.

III   Set up a conference room: *As you think about being relaxed
and comfortable as you sit in the director's chair at this meeting,
I'd like you to invite into the room, one at a time, the skills and
strengths you think will help you. What skill would walk in
first?*

III   Developing resources and their images: *As each skill or
strength walks in, you ask what it is and what form or image or
person represents that skill or strength: courage = lion, strength
= the Hulk, intelligence = a big brain or Einstein, and so forth.*

(I often ask them if they want to ask for skills that I think they need, but I rarely chime in on what the form should be.)

||| *Focus on your team and the skills and strengths they have. What feelings and emotions are you beginning to experience as you look at your team? Where do you feel that? What posture would you have, sitting in your director's chair as you look at your team? As you feel that posture, what do you notice now?*

||| With each strength, move through this script: *Think of a time when you used your inner "Hulk" and it worked for you. When you think of that time, what emotions and body feelings do you notice?* If the feelings are positive: *Think of how you can use your inner "Hulk" in your current life. What's a particular situation he can help with? Imagine that.*

||| Bringing all the resources together:

   | *As director, ask each strength if it's willing to work with the others on your behalf.*

   | *Bring them all together, and bring them inside. Where will you feel them in your body? What's it feel like?*

   | *What will you name your team?*

   | *What symbol will stand for your whole team? Think of a way to wear or carry that symbol or see that symbol.* (People can use it as wallpaper on their phones or desktops, as jewelry, on the front of their datebooks, etc.)

   | *Imagine using your team in your daily life:*
      - *First, think of going through the ordinary irritations and setbacks of an ordinary day. How do you deal with those?*
      - *Now think of handling those distressing times.* (The ones that cause big regressed blowups, meltdowns, and disintegration.) *Call on the team, feel them inside, and put*

> *them in charge. How is it when you have your strong Hulk,*
> *your brilliant Einstein, your stubborn ox, your heartful*
> *and patient Dalai Lama, and your resourceful Oprah tak-*
> *ing care of business?*
>   – *Imagine your angry, suicidal inside teenager arises. How*
>   *can this team keep her safe and calm her down?*
>   – *Let's go through each inside part and introduce them to*
>   *your team.*

||| Closure: *Let's write down each strength and its corresponding*
symbol and then the group name and the symbol on this card.
You can carry it in your wallet and always have access to your
group.

Using Religious, Spiritual, or Other Experiences of Support

People who have an experience of a loving, powerful, and protective deity or spiritual connection have an already built-in resource
ready to be tapped. Here are some examples:

||| *What parts of you have the most connection to God? How do*
you experience that? (If it's a positive experience) *Can you*
expand that to every part of every age of you? Can you feel the
love/power/wisdom coming through you? What parts of you
need an extra dose?

||| *Can you feel the love/nurturing/power of Jesus/the Virgin*
(especially for Hispanic Catholics)/*God/the Goddess/your*
guru/your Higher Power (Alcoholics Anonymous and like
groups) *come into all the parts of you? Breathe that through*
your body and all your ages. Use the neural pathways that are
already there, to enhance the function of specific or all ego

states. Remember, this is not about converting anyone to anything; it's about using existing resources (adapted from Milton Erickson, in Haley, 1973).

Using Positive States

Have your clients imagine access to and act from their grown-up, skilled, functional selves. "Future pace" (neurolinguistic programming term) situations that will arise and how they'll handle it. Possible situations can include the following:

III Getting tasks done: *Imagine that it's morning and you're overwhelmed with all you should do. What part of you is up to organizing the tasks and getting at them? Imagine going inside and locating that smart, skilled adult. Imagine the tasks and getting to them, one at a time.*

III Nurturing inside (for more dissociative clients): *Imagine that the devastating loneliness overtakes you. Which grown-up parts can connect with those lonely kid parts, hold them, and let them know that there's an adult around? Imagine the comforting presence of that adult part taking care of the kid parts. Let's find that adult and practice taking care of those little ones inside.*

III Protecting: *Imagine walking down that scary street. Do you want that scared kid or that strong adult who can see danger and know whether to confront it or run like hell? Imagine, before you start walking, you bring your oldest, strongest you into that body. You're walking tall. You're grounded. You're not a target. Imagine walking through without a problem . . . Imagine walking through and having to confront someone . . .*

> *Now imagine walking through, realizing it's not safe, and*
> *you need to run, and choosing the safest haven with your adult*
> *brain.*

III Knowing what's really going on: *What part of you could*
make the best assessment of the situation, that scared (angry
or helpless, etc.) child part of you or that smart adult techie?
Imagine, when you're in that meeting, bringing your techie up
to scope out what's happening and responding from him. Imag-
ine not being silent and not being the kind of jerk that would
lose you your job. Imagine yourself being that smart, adult guy.
What would that be like? How will that adult keep that child
contained during the meeting? Let's walk through it.

The Two-Hand Technique

Clients often need help differentiating one thing from another:
the safe present time from the traumatic past; adult capacity from
childlike ignorance and helplessness; feelings of alarm from real
danger; and the feeling of being drawn more to one decision over
another. I developed the two-hand technique (Shapiro, 2005b)
years ago to help clients in these determinations. It is body-
based, so it brings sensation into the thoughts about differences.
It physicalizes "on the one hand this, and the other hand that."
Often, the "states" that it delineates are less than full-blown. It
can used for finding and delineating ego states.

1. Have your client place a different ego state in each hand.
2. Delineate the differences, with physical, emotional, and
   other state-specific traits.
3. Facilitate an interaction between the two. Keep the client

accessing internally by asking feeling, sensing, wondering, or thinking questions.

Here is an example of how you might use the two-hand technique:

> *Which hand is that terrified little girl in? Can you feel how small she is? Can you get a sense of her thoughts and her real vulnerability? Now find your oldest, wisest, strongest self. Hold that grown-up part in your other hand. Feel how much bigger she is than that little girl. Can you feel her strength? Feel her wisdom? Feel her competency? Notice the resources that she has. Notice what she would do, as a competent adult, if she were in that situation. Bring the adult hand over to that little girl hand. Hold that little girl. Let her know that you are there. Let her feel surrounded with your strength, your competence, and your resources. Tell her that she lives with you now. Take her on a tour of your adult life: your job, your house, and your children. Let her see all the people who love you in your adult life. Let her see what a good parent you are and how well you take care of little girls. Let her know that you are going to handle this situation. It's your job, not hers. How's that little girl now? Where's that little girl now? Is she still in your hand? (The client often reports that she's "inside" now. If not:) Where is that little girl going to live so that you can take care of her from here on in, and she can know that she's always got you to take care of her?*

Don't force integration. Rigidly dissociated fragments of traumatic experience will often integrate naturally with this method. It is useful with DID after much of the trauma work is done. I've seen pieces integrate after I suggested, *Put the four-year-old that saw the abuse in one hand and the four-year-old that felt the feelings in the other. Are they ready to come to together now? Great, bring those hands together. What's happening with those parts? They've come together? How does that feel?* Of course, if it's easy to find and delineate states or if integration occurs naturally after clearing trauma, you don't need this technique.

POSITIVE STATES: WRAPPING UP

Whatever your clients' situations, they need access to their oldest, wisest, and most functional states. Effective psychotherapy happens in the connection between resourced adult states and dysfunctional, often younger ones. You may simply ask, *What age goes with that? Can we get your adult in the room to help us with it?* You may have to do a more elaborate intervention to bring up and flesh out a functional, present adult state. Either way, you will see better function and faster healing with the healthiest parts of your clients running the show.

CHAPTER 3

Foundational Intervention: Creating Safe Places and Internal Caregivers

"Safe place" exercises are ubiquitous in psychotherapy, yoga, and many spiritual practices. They are helpful as preparation for trauma work (mandatory for eye movement desensitization and reprocessing [EMDR]; Shapiro, 2001) and essential for working with highly dissociated ego states. In safe places, because they are out of ordinary life, it is often helpful to use external figures for protection and attachment. Safe places may include attachment or protective figures. With dissociative clients, some preexisting, no-longer-functional protectors can be realigned to present-day needs and situations.

BASIC SAFE PLACE INTERVENTION

1. Have clients think about a place that's safe and brings a feeling of comfort. If they are having trouble thinking of a real place, have them make one up.

2. Have them tell you what makes it safe.
3. Have them imagine being there, looking around, feeling the peacefulness. (*Hear the wind in the trees around the cabin, notice the quality of the light and how snug and safe you feel, being there.*) If they feel good and relaxed there, great. If they don't feel safe and relaxed, ask what needs to change. Work on it until you and they get it right.
4. Have them imagine visualizing the safe place when settling into bed or when distressed.

HEALING PLACE FOR TRAUMATIZED CLIENTS

For clients who can't recall experiences of safety (many abuse survivors), the idea of safety may be distressing, so we change the name to "healing place" and build in deeper safety. Explain this healing place with lots of pauses for them to visualize and feel the experience.

> *Imagine a healing place that is invisible to everyone but you. It can be on a seashore, in a forest, on a mountain, in the desert, or any place you want. To make it completely safe—it can even be off planet. What did you pick? What makes it healing? Wander around it and make sure that it suits you. You can change anything you want, because it's yours. No one else has a way in but you. Make sure there's a house or cabin (or, in the case of polyfragmented DID clients, a mansion or condominium building with a room for each full-blown part). Let's walk through the house and notice how it's furnished, what kind of windows there are, what makes it secure, and what makes it healing. There's the kitchen. What's it like? Make sure you have a magic refrigerator and magic cup-*

*boards with food that you adore, especially comfort food. There are
no calories in the healing place.*

*(For sexual abuse survivors:) Let's explore the bedroom. How
many locks are there on the inside of the door? How is the bed different from the bed that you had as a child? What makes it safe and
healing? Let's walk the grounds. What do you see? Do you need an
invisible containment field around the perimeter and overhead?
Great, then do it. Figure out where you're going to put the healing
pool. And when we work with inner children, what will they need
here? (A swing set, a dog, a sandbox, toys, etc.) Make it so! Later
on, in therapy or at home, if it ever gets too overwhelming, you can
take a break and visit this healing place.*

SAFE PLACE WITH ATTACHMENT FIGURES

Adult clients are often able to find the nurturing and protective parts of themselves and then take care of younger or less
functional parts. Most of the examples in this book use this
kind of internal or "self" figure. Some clients' adult parts are
highly avoidant or "phobic" (van der Hart et al., 2006) of their
younger parts or EPs (emotional parts). Some, feeling their EPs
as unwanted intrusions on their "normal" lives, want to erad-
icate those parts. And some clients, while not exactly phobic,
do not have the protective or attachment skills to adequately
care for their inner kids. With these clients, it is necessary to
bring outside protectors and nurturers into their safe or healing places.

For clients with attachment issues, create an attachment figure for the safe place, and begin to lay down new attachment
connections in their brains:

If you could have any being you wanted, someone or something to watch over you, protect you, and always be ready to respond lovingly to you, 24/7, who or what would you want in the healing place? (People choose Jesus, Mary, a bodhisattva, the Dalai Lama, Obi-Wan from Star Wars, a bear, the Super Nanny from television, angels, a generic good grandmother, their best friend's great mother, Wonder Woman, or others.)

Imagine that you get lonely. Let that angel hold you. Imagine that you get scared. How will that angel protect you and comfort you? Stand guard with a sword? How will it comfort you? Hugs? Close your eyes and imagine the angel's arms and wings surrounding you. What's that like? Breathe in that sense of safety and connectedness. (Highly dissociated clients may have a room and a different protector for every part. As the parts make themselves known, each can find a place to stay and a custom-made nurturing and protective figure.)

How old is this piece of you? What was going on in his life? . . . He's four, scared, lonely, and is the part that remembers the abuse. It sounds like he's going to need to feel safe, to know that the scary stuff is over, and to feel loved all the time. What kind of room does he need? A playroom with a loft bed, so no one can reach him . . . What a brilliant solution! You and he look around the room. Notice the quality of the light. Notice what makes it safe. See the toys? What's the best one?

What kind of being does he need in the room? A big bear sounds great. Make sure it's friendly to him and very protective of him and never, ever scares or hurts him. (An abuser may have been friendly but not protected him.) Let's bring him up to this room now and get him oriented to this new, safe place. What does he think? . . . I'm so glad he likes it! Introduce him to the bear. Can the bear pick him up? What happens when the bear looks at him with crinkly, happy eyes? He likes that, too? What kind of feeling does he have inside when he looks at the bear and it has happy eyes for him? It makes me feel good, when he feels good inside. (Notice how we enhanced attachment circuitry, by having him feel his connection to the attachment object and have his affect reflected by me.)

This is a magic bear. It never has to sleep, so it's always standing guard. It always is available to respond to any happy feeling or any sad or scared feeling. If the four-year-old is angry, the bear won't be scared away. This mama bear can take it, stay present, and love that kid, no matter what! When your little boy wants to play by himself, the bear will be in the corner. When he wants to be held, the bear will be there for a cuddle. And no <u>one</u> or no <u>thing</u> will bother that boy with that bear around. When your four-year-old thinks that the people who hurt him are around, the bear will be there to make sure they stay away and that the little boy knows that things are different now.

Later, when your four-year-old is feeling safe, and loved, and lovable, we'll introduce him to the other kids and the other parts of the house. In the meantime, you can make any changes you need to, to the room and the bear, to make it safe, and easy.

(To speed up the process create a continual experience of safe, nurturing containment:) *Every moment that your grown-up parts are working, taking care of things, or entertaining themselves, and every moment that your grown-up parts are asleep, this child part of yours is safe, held, and being responded to, just the way he always needed.* (I am indebted to David Calof for this final part of the intervention.)

Occasionally, clients with seemingly intractable insomnia begin to sleep by imagining themselves in their healing places, being watched over or held by their healing place attachment object.

SAFE PLACE FOR A CLIENT'S
REJECTED OR DENIED PARTS

When a client initially rejects a part, we can find the part a good place and a good protective/nurturing figure and add some safeguards.

> *You don't want to hold this child part, and you think she's the cause of the problem. It sounds like all the experiences and emotions that she's carrying are overwhelming to the rest of you. Let's put her someplace safe and leak-proof, so that the grown-up you can function.*

Joanne Twombly (2005) suggests making the place soundproof and feeling-proof, to keep the distressed parts' intolerable feelings from intruding on the functional adult part.

> *We're putting a magic filter around the room. All of that child's distressing feelings, and images, and emotions will rise straight up and dissipate into the universe. None of them can ooze into any other room or any other part of you. All week long, the adult part of you can go about your business. When you come to my office, we'll check in on this little girl and see how she's doing and if she needs anything. In the meantime, she's got a loving, protective grandmother, all the kid food she wants, and lots of toys. When she's feeling miserable, the grandmother will take care of her. When she's happy, the grandmother will laugh with her. This part of you will*

be healing in the safe place every minute of every day, even when you're asleep. I wonder how she'll be next week, after a week of rest and play and healing . . .

(In case you haven't noticed, this intervention, like all safe place interventions, is a hypnotic induction.)

SAFE AND HEALING PLACES WITH ORGANIZED ABUSE CLIENTS

Safe places and healing places may be hard to use with survivors of ritual abuse or other forms of mind control. These clients were coerced, often with torture or drugs, into dissociative responses, sometimes with parts organized into different kinds of "rooms" in an imagined structure. While some people may resist the idea of a safe place because "it's too airy-fairy, woo-woo," ritual abuse/mind control clients may panic or get way too compliant when you bring up the idea. With these cases, go slowly, and take pains to differentiate what you are doing from what happened before. Get permission from each known part. And because these people are often very fragmented, you may need to take each separate part on a tour of the new healing place.

Parts that are identified with the perpetrators' organization or parts that believe that a sense of safety is dangerous may try to destroy the healing place. (I have seen it with my clients and heard about many other instances.) These parts may be patiently, but firmly, led, by other stronger parts, at your suggestion, to safe, comfortable rooms adjacent to the healing place, where they are taken care of and may not harm the healing place or other parts. Sometimes, Twombly's (2005) "soundproof, feeling-proof room" is necessary for these parts, for a while.

You may want other special features in the safe place for these kinds of clients:

⦀ Specialized "switching places" for sorting the destructive and nondestructive parts.

⦀ A healing pool for soaking off pain and detritus from abuse (useful with many sexually abused clients, especially DID ones).

⦀ Souped-up security—some clients imagine all kinds of weaponry pointed outward. Many have been happiest when we took the whole thing "off planet." People who specialize in these kinds of cases have layers of tricky "entrances" into the safe places.

⦀ Souped-up internal security for clients to deal with parts identified with the abusive organization, or other destructive parts.

(These suggestions came from other people, who would like to remain anonymous.)

CASE EXAMPLE Safe Place With a Reluctant Adult Self

Jenny was a smart, functional professional and mother who, at six-weeks-old, had been separated from her ailing mother for two weeks. During that time she had been mostly ignored by her over-whelmed, attachment-impaired father and had grown strong states (trying hard, rage, despair, and shutdown) that had grown into parts of her at different ages. She had been hospitalized many times as a teenager and young adult (when her younger rage, despair, and shut-down states had taken over) and had been given a variety of diagnoses and medications. When, in an early session with me, her despairing younger part arose and swamped the intelligent, functional part of her, I attempted to get the adult part back into the room. She was curled up, wailing, and not responsive.

Jenny, quick, tell me the ages of your boys! What grades are they in?
Um, um . . . Six and three. The six-year-old is in first grade.

Okay, Ms. Adult who knows she has kids. It's nice to see you front and center. Look around the room, then look over at me. Do I look familiar?
Yeah, I know you.

Great. Do you know what happened?
Not really. I freaked out and was keeled over on the couch, but I don't know why.

When I asked you a question, it took you back to a baby part of you, and it took a little work to bring back this adult part. I'd like to teach you some ways to take care of this baby part, so you can stay in the here and now, when you want to.
No way! This shit has been ruining my life, and I don't want anything to do with it! I don't want to go there at all. (Quite the phobia of dissociative parts!)

I gotcha. Then I want to try something else. Let me set up a holding situation for these kid parts of you, so that you don't have to deal with their intrusions into grown-up life. Does that sound okay?

I guess.

So can I get you to imagine a place, far away from here, that would be a safe, comfortable place for kids? (She nods.) *A place where there are caregivers who are like the best moms on Earth: always available, always kind and protective, and with the strongest, softest arms that people could have. This place is the best day care center on Earth, and it's absolutely free.*
Sounds cool.

Let's bring that wailing, despairing baby here and put her right into the arms of the warmest, most connecting caregiver. She can bring that baby into a lovely nursery with soothing colors and soft light, and she can hold that baby in a big rocking chair, looking into her eyes and cooing sweet words. This baby, and any other distressing parts of you, can be in this place as long as you need them to, being cared for, fed, held, changed, and comforted, every second that your adult self is doing whatever needs to happen in your adult life . . . How does that work for you?
Much better!

Can you check in with those caregivers on a daily basis, to see how it's going?
I can do that, if I don't have to see those scary kids.

That works.

Over several weeks, several ages and moods of Jenny were checked into the safe place. As we built up Jenny's adult self and her capacity for affect tolerance, she became more curious about her other parts. A few months later, I asked her if she wanted to peak into the Best Day Care Center (the name for her safe place) and check on the littlest ones. The baby that had been despairing was calm, connectable, and gurgling. Jenny imagined picking her up and hugging her. She felt her as separate, not herself, but bearable. We set up daily ten-minute "visits" with that baby and other baby parts, all of whom were healing and starting to melt into one baby. Jenny found that she was losing less time to being in disconnected states, and was less forgetful and less anxious. A year later, she could be with all her small child parts. Two years later, after much ego state work, EMDR, and problem solving, all parts, including the hell-raising teenage addict, were tolerable and containable by the adult Jenny part. Jenny's adult was then able to send acting-out parts to the day care, when necessary, and pull them out to debrief later.

WHEN PREEXISTING PROTECTIVE PARTS ARE DYSFUNCTIONAL

Traumatized brains have many ways of protecting people from further injury. They can use anxiety to turn up the physical sense of danger. The amygdala can trigger pictures, sensations, and thoughts that went with past trauma. If the trauma was recurrent, and especially if it started early, our brains can give us protective "parts" to keep us from harm. The more dissociative we are, the more fleshed-out and complex the "protectors."

Often "protector" parts do not appear protective. They can use the same abuse techniques that external abusers used. After unzipping the loud abusers, more than one client told me, "He

is hurting me the way my dad did, so my dad won't hurt me."
Preexisting dissociative protectors

III   can be gentle, nice, and kind and simply remind or take
care of other parts;
III   can be belligerent, but only to outside people;
III   can be the "critic" voice inside a person;
III   can be abusive to inside parts; or
III   can be nice but too avoidant or otherwise dysfunctional for
the client's current life.

In DID, unspecified dissociative disorders, and some extreme
PTSD clients, preexisting dissociative protectors may take over
the body in order to protect, sometimes with disastrous results.
(It's not good to hit your pretty-nice boss who is correcting your
punctuation.)

In victims of organized abuse, whether ritual abuse or mind
control, "protectors" may actually be protecting the abusive organization, not the client, and may need to be deactivated. When
these are "unzipped," they sometimes disappear or show themselves to be more identified with the abusive organization than
your individual client.

Unzipping dysfunctional protectors

1.   Identify the part. *Go inside, and find out what part is doing
that.*
2.   Find the zipper or other method for going inside the protector. I've used zippers or "going inside the inside part": *I want
you to imagine that you can see inside that big, belligerent part*

of you. Notice if there's another part inside . . . ? What is that inside part? How old? What was going on in his life when he got inside the big one? How was that fighter helping then? Is that a function you need in your current life?

3. Find what the client needed the protector for.
4. Have the adult part of the client explain, or better yet, show the protector that times have changed and that the need for that kind of protection is over.
5. Reassign, integrate, or give a long-deserved vacation or nap to the protector part.

CASE EXAMPLE **Working With a Protector**

This client is avoidant of new experiences, especially anything involving risk.

Go inside and notice what part of you avoids trying anything new?
It's really big and really strong and angry and criticizes me all the time.

How old does this part feel to you?
It's adult. Maybe not as old as me, but grown up.

What's its job?
Its job is to keep me from failing.

When did it first show up in your life?
I've heard this voice inside for a long time.

Is it someone else's voice, perhaps a parent's?

No. It's me.

Do me a favor, and imagine walking to the back of the big, strong, angry protector . . . Look for the zipper protruding out the back of the head and running down the back, all the way to the ground.
I see it. That's weird.

Grab that zipper, and unzip it all the way to the ground . . . What do you see there?
I see this little kid me, surrounded by this big me who is supposed to protect me from failure, by keeping me from trying anything.

Sort of like the little guy running the Great Oz in the Wizard of Oz?
Exactly like him.

What was he protecting you from, by keeping you from failing?
He protected me from my big brother's criticism and my mom being sad and the other kids making fun of me for coming up with the crazy ideas to do stuff.

Could you thank this child for trying to protect you for so many years?
Really?!

He was trying to do well by you and keep you from social harm. He's a good kid.
Okay. Thanks little guy, for trying to keep me from looking like a fool.

Do you continue to need that kind of management?
No. I can avoid the bad stuff, but use some more of my creative brain without the constant self-criticism.

It's nice being an adult, who knows the difference . . . That kid has been working a long time, do you think he could use some time off for good behavior? (He nods.) *Could you bring him up to right now and show him around and have this kid notice how things have changed? What will you show this child?*
I live with a great, supportive woman, in a nice house. I'm safe now. There's no kind of failure I could do that's really dangerous. My friends are supportive. (He starts to smile.) I think I was terrorized into knocking back my creative part, because of this part of me. This kid is starting to morph back into the zany, creative kid that I used to be! This is going to be fun!

CASE EXAMPLE A Protector in a Dissociative Client

After many years of therapy for his dissociative symptoms after horrifically violent abuse from his parents, every time Gary began to feel safe and comfortable about himself, his head would hurt and his ears would buzz. His suicidal ideation was gone. He functioned beautifully at work and as a father. He could finally nearly look me straight in the eye, without looking down. His long, deep depression was starting to lift. But he still couldn't entertain the possibility that he was a good man. We had tried talking to the headache, tried finding the part that caused it; I tried every intervention I knew, to no avail. One day, when the headache was beginning, I handed Gary a notebook and a pen.

Can you let that part write or draw what it's trying to communicate to you? Whatever is there, let it come through.
(Gary's hand wavers over the paper. His hand finally draws a small picture of a man using his pelvis to push a child into a wall, an instance of abuse by his father.)

What's that part saying about that abuse?
(He then draws an equals sign and then a slanted line through it.)

Does not equal.
(He draws a sideways oval.)

Is that a halo? The abuse does not equal an angel?
(Gary shakes his head.)

Being abused means you can't be good?
(Another head shake. Then he redraws the equals sign, without the strike through.)

If you know you're good, you will be abused?
(After a pause, he nods sadly.)

This little part of you that has been protecting you from harm still holds that you caused the abuse and that your narcissistic asshole father will abuse you again if you lift your head up and feel good.
(Another nod.)

Gary, I know we've used this with other parts of you, but not with this one. Can we use Jim Knipe's shame technique with this little one? (He nods.) *Do you have enough adult around to do it?* (Another nod.)

Feel that part of you that takes care of your kids at home, that piece of you that protects them, responds to them, drives them around, and is the opposite of the father you had. You're there? Good. How old is that headache kid? Put your pen on the paper and draw a number, and I bet we'll have it.

(Gary draws a big wavy 4 on the page.)

So this is a four-year-old. He's been doing this hard job for a long, long time. Can you, from your good father place, thank this child part of you for working so hard, for so long to protect you.

Thank you, little one. (He then sighs.)

Can you bring that child up here?

(Gary begins to space out and then shakes his head.)

Gary, wait! I have an idea. Can you draw a few things from this office into the picture? Draw your chair. It doesn't have to be art. Then me in my chair. Then draw this rug you've seen hundreds of times. Great. Can this kid see this room in his space? Can you draw a big circle of safety around it? Good. Is that child in this year in this room? Good. Take another sheet, and draw a big rectangle movie screen on it. Draw you and the little protector boy watching the screen. Now imagine you are watching a quick run-through of that particular abuse event with your dad. We know what the kid sees. It's happened because he let down his guard and thought he was okay. What does your grown-up good father part think? Say it, and then draw it.

My father was evil and a psychopath who enjoyed inflicting pain on me. I was a little kid.

Does this four-year-old get it?

No.

Then draw it
(Gary draws a little picture of his father and then draws horns
and a tail on him. He draws another picture of the child, a very
tiny child, and draws the halo over his head.) Little one, he was
the devil. It was never your fault. It was never our fault. And you
don't keep us safe by hurting us. (Gary crosses out the two pictures of his father.) And we haven't seen him in fourteen years
and will never, ever see him . . . It's okay to know we're safe.

What's happening?
I don't know. He's processing this.

Draw something in the present.
(On a new sheet, Gary draws a house with four stick figures
and a stick dog [his family]. He draws the Space Needle. [He
lives in Seattle.] And he draws a big circle around it all.) This
is where we live now, and it's safe to be safe. And it's safe to
be good, and know we're good.

How's that kid doing?
It's starting to sink in for the first time. No headache. No ear
ringing. It's hard to believe!

And how is that kid?
He's tired.

Can you hold him?

No, but I can draw him. (Gary draws a small stick boy sleeping in the arms of a big stick man, himself. Then he draws the man hugging the boy, then a smiling man, alone.)

In many years of therapy, as we had processed trauma and assimilated every other major part, this four-year-old protector had remained vigilant. If Gary felt happy, relieved, or a glimmer of pride, this part brought on ear ringing, headaches, and nausea. Its belief was that positive affect showed that Gary existed, and that his existence was the reason for the abuse. As a result, Gary had almost no sense of pride or normal human entitlement. In the months that followed, we worked at Gary holding my gaze, saying "no" to me and others in his life, and owning his accomplishments, including raising great kids, doing good work, and surviving his awful childhood to stay alive and healing until the present moment.

USING SAFE PLACES

Safe place exercises are ubiquitous in psychotherapy. Google lists over three hundred thousand references to them. Some clients with high affect tolerance, no dissociation, or no imagination don't need them. Traumatized, poorly attached, and or dissociative clients can use their safe places to build a sense of calm and safety, shift their states, nurture and mature younger parts, and protect their ANPs from constant traumatic intrusion.

CHAPTER 4

Foundational Intervention: Working With Infant and Child States

Babies form bonds with the people and beings around them, building a separate neural network with its own set of responses for every recurring person or situation. Singular emotionally intense situations, whether very good or horrific, also create neural tracks. When early attachment goes well, children learn to expect kindness, consistency, and good attention from other people. When consistently responded to, children grow their own capacities for self-soothing, tolerating feelings, and knowing that they are safe, important, and worth the good treatment that they receive (Schore, 1994; Siegel, 1999). When children are inconsistently responded to, abused, or neglected or have "scary" depressed, angry, addicted, or dissociated parents, their brains grow wide neural pathways for anxiety, fear, shame, dissociation, and rigid defenses against these feeling states.

Child states: Healthy resources

||| Infant states in a well-attached, nontraumatized person can be happy, connected, and sure of being protected. Call on these states as resources for a newly traumatized or humiliated adult client. *You may not remember this, but you may be able to feel that happy little girl you were when you were held in your parents' arms, while they admired your baby presence. What do you notice inside when you think about that part of you? Was that baby lovable? Was she safe? Can you feel that knowledge inside of you?*

||| April Steele (2007b) has an exercise called "Adventuring Spirit" in which she directs a client's adult part to hold the toddler part, let him wander away to play, admire the playing, and then greet and hold the toddler again. The toddler part sees, feels, and hears the adult as the adult part sees, feels, and hears the toddler. This work can build more secure attachment, vanquish separation anxiety, and shift people from passive behavior to taking charge of their lives.

||| Children are programmed to be curious explorers and problem solvers. When saddled with an anxious or controlling caregiver, inhibited by abuse or internal anxiety, or made to live in an ill-fitting social box, they can dampen that curiosity in favor of fitting in or avoiding abuse. Rekindle the "explorer" part of inhibited, anxious, or depressed adult clients: *Can you go inside and find that little girl who is curious about her surroundings and wants to figure out how everything works? What age is she? What kinds of things interest her? . . . She's eight and she loves nature, animals, and bugs. If you can scan through your current life with her, where would she most like to go? . . . When can you take*

her to the zoo? . . . Before then, do you think she and you might watch a nature show on TV? . . . You're smiling. Can you and your inside kid experience the promise to have some joy together before the next session?

Dysfunctional child states

||| *Attachment-impaired states.* When babies don't receive loving, appropriate responses from caregivers, they may develop deep neural pathways/states for every emotion they have been stuck in. This can happen with disruptions in good attachment, such as a separation from good parents or with impaired caregivers, who might be grieving, addicted, overwhelmed, or simply clueless about responding to children. People with poor attachment may live in or switch between desperate yearning states to "seductive," angry, spaced-out, and shame states. Or they may develop "dismissive" (Bowlby, 1969, 1973), "I don't need anyone" defensive states. (See Chapter 7 on personality disorders for more on these issues.)

||| *Trauma states.* If a single trauma is intense enough, it can cause a dissociative event in a child. The rape or severe beating of a child can create a split between the physical experience, the emotional experience, and the sense of watching it from the ceiling. If trauma is repetitive, these splits may move from "states" to full-grown dissociative parts. In either case, traumatized children will be more easily triggered and rendered dysfunctional by later traumas. These clients will often seem overanxious, overcontrolling, too angry, or too shut down in response to current circumstances.

||| *Social distress.* Many of us carry some social fears from
childhood. Think about walking into a new consult group.
Would you have any anxiety about how you are seen by
your peers? Is any of that left over from your social experiences in school? On the playground? In the neighborhood?
When children are bullied, shunned, or publicly shamed,
they may develop social reflexes and social persona ranging
from "hunkering down" or overaccommodation to social
avoidance or extreme control. When as adults, or even as
older children, their social group changes for the better,
their behavior may be stuck in the earlier learned states.

Many ego states are created in childhood. Most ego state
therapies focus on healing and integrating child "parts" that
are dysfunctional for the present time. Some, like April Steele's
(2007a) imaginal nurturing, focus specifically on infant and toddler states.

Ego state work brings mature and functional rationality,
affect regulation, experience, reparative nurturing, and containment to child states that need them. To attain that goal, therapists help clients to bring the neural networks of the oldest and
wisest, most nurturing, or most stable states into contact with the
younger, more traumatized, or more rigid neural networks.

CASE EXAMPLE Using Current Adult Capacities to Protect and Nurture

Grady was thirty-seven, had tattoos on his muscled arms, rode a
motorcycle, and seemed always ready for battle. He had a childhood of tremendous neglect and trauma and had come to ther-

apy to deal with his relationship-killing aggression, which arose from PTSD-based trauma and shame. He could banter but rarely allowed true connection. His dismissive attachment style would not let him acknowledge the terror and shame that underlay his issues. Strategically, I enlisted his "warrior" role as protector of all his kid parts.

Grady, have you ever held a baby?
Yeah. I had a little brother, six years younger, and I've held other people's kids over the years.

What would you do if someone tried to hurt a kid that you knew?
Beat the crap out of them (angrily).

What would you tell a kid that got hurt?
(Grady looks at the floor, sighs, and then looks up.) It won't happen again, if I'm around (sternly).

Would you tell that kid that you were sorry it happened?
Yeah (sadly).

Would you tell that kid he didn't deserve it?
Of course! He's just a kid.

Grady, let's use this wonderful protector part of you to take care of that kid inside of you. Could you go back in time to one of those times when you were a kid and your stepdad beat you up, and pick up that little boy?

(Grady held his breath for a moment, nods, and then shuts his eyes. A few minutes later, he looks much softer.)
I got him

Great! How old is this one?
Six.

Feel his weight in your arms . . . Have him feel your strong arms holding him . . . Look into his eyes . . . And have that kid look back and see that you're 100 percent there for him . . . Notice what it's like to hold that kid while he notices that he's being held by a strong, safe guy (adapted from Steele, 2007a).
(Grady tears up. His big shoulders drop as he sighs.)

Now fly him up, over all the years, to right now. Watch those years and all that stuff go by, like you're in a fast jet, just flying over. Are you and that kid here and now? (This is a variation on life span integration [Pace, 2007].)
    Is that kid feeling safe, now? Good. So let's talk to him. Tell him that he's safe with you . . . (he nods) *that it wasn't his fault . . . that he's a good kid . . . and that he lives with you now . . . Tell him that it's safe to feel stuff now . . . and that you have people around who aren't assholes. Show him where you live, who's around, and that your stepfather is nowhere in your life . . . How's that kid?*
Better!

What's different?
He knows he's okay.

How are you feeling?
Weird. I'm lighter in some way. And feel safer. This stuff is strange. But cool.

How often should you check in with that inside kid, let him know that you're around, and see what he needs?
At least every day. I'll talk to him when I go to bed at night, and anytime something freaky happens.

What freaky things will you be looking out for?
I'd say that if people are angry, or if something bad happens, or if I'm just feeling stuff, I should check in.

How can this kid part of you get your attention, when he needs it?
I'll feel it, right here. (He thumps his chest.)

Imagine feeling it and responding to that inside kid.
Got it (nodding).

This session was a turning point for Grady. Over the weeks, as we "flew up" different parts, including his internal baby and his reactive, rage-filled teen, he gained tolerance for his affect, including vulnerability. Five weeks after the first ego state session, we began working directly on his suspicion of other people.

Grady, when you feel like pushing people away, what age are you?
Most of them.

Could you be more specific?

Maybe . . . school age, but probably younger.

Is there a rule about that?
Most people are assholes, and you can't trust them.

You came by that belief honestly! Now that you're thirty-seven, have you ever met people who aren't assholes?
Yeah, I know a few.

How does that adult you tell the difference?
By what they do and how they do it. People who tell the truth and treat other people okay, are okay. People who don't are assholes.

That works for me. Here's the deal: I think your younger parts are treating everyone, even the okay people, like they're assholes, because that's who they were used to being around. We have to get your adult guy in charge of connecting with other people, because he can tell the good ones from the jerks. He can even tell when a normally good one is being a temporary jerk. Are you ready to do this? (Grady stops breathing and shrinks down in his chair.) I don't know. I feel weird.

What parts are feeling weird?
Most of the kids think we're going to get creamed.

Does this explain anything?
I get it. This is why I'm avoiding everyone.

Okay, Mr. Thirty-Seven-Year-Old Grady, front and center!

Yes, ma'am!

I want you to start at infancy, and sweep up every single age inside of you, coming up all the years. Spread those big strong arms, and sweep up the kids, year by year: first that baby you, then that toddler, that preschooler, the kindergartner, all the years in grade school, junior high, high school, first job, all the years until right now . . . Got them all?
Got 'em!

Who is in charge?
I am.

Tell them . . . Who is going to keep them safe?
Me.

Who is going to pick out safe people to connect with?
I am.

And who is going to keep the younger kids from avoiding the nice people and the teenager from actively shoving them away?
That would be me.

Great!! I want you to imagine that you meet a guy who could be a friend. Maybe he likes bikes, and the same music, or maybe he's different than you. Imagine that you, as your adult, assess him for assholeness and that he passes your test. The kids are scared and want to avoid him. Imagine talking inside to calm them down and then sweeping them back behind you, saying, It's okay, I'll handle this.

(Grady closes his eyes, and runs through the scenario, sweeping his hand back, then sighing. He looks over at me.) I can do this.

In other sessions, we worked similarly with his issues with women, bosses, and conflict. The more the adult Grady took care of the inside kids, the more functional, connected, and differentiated he became in all of his relationships.

WORKING WITH CHILD STATES

Child ego states can be tied to positive or negative emotions, useful life skills, reflexive dissociative states (that were always useful, when created), and the degree of power and control that people had, earlier in life. In therapy, people can rediscover their playful, inventive, joyful early selves and start having much more fun. They start by rounding up their lost, ashamed, powerless, or terrified younger parts and introduce them to the present, safer, more supportive reality. When these parts are dissociated from current reality, clients can experience disruption in decision making, affect, or behavior. If dissociated parts have been holding experiences that were too distressing for the adult ANP to handle, clients can be in for awful surprises when the parts come forward with their experiences. In therapy, the trauma is healed and the parts are integrated.

CASE EXAMPLE Working With Dissociative Infant
States in an Older Child

During Sheila's difficult birth, her mother hemorrhaged and nearly died. Baby Sheila was taken to a noisy, impersonal neonatal ward and mostly ignored for five days. Evidently, her baby consciousness split into several nearly exclusive states. At twelve years old Sheila, despite having a devoted, attached mother, was barely able to leave her mother's side and switched rapidly among angry, anxious, clinging, and spaced-out states. Her diagnoses included borderline personality disorder, obsessive-compulsive disorder, and dissociative disorders, not otherwise specified.

During three years of therapy, we used every tool in my therapeutic toolbox. For the first four months she would start every session with her face buried in her mother's lap. Our first task was to find her twelve-year-old state:

Hey, you! Can I talk to that twelve-year-old, the one who goes to middle school?
Okay.
(We discuss current events in her life, in order to solidify her most mature state, and then go to work.)

Okay, Miss Twelve, what age goes with that part of you that got so scared when your mom went out last night?
The five-year-old.

Any other ages?
And the baby.

Let's go get them, baby first. What's up with her?
She's scared! And then she's mad.

What's she need from you?
To not be alone.

So can you go find that baby and pick her up, just like you picked up your little sister?
Yes!

Let her feel your arms around her . . . And your mom's arms around you right now. (Mom hugs her more snugly.) *Look into that baby's eyes. What's that baby feeling now?*
Sad! . . . Now she's mad . . .

And you're still here? (I'm checking for the twelve-year-old ego state in a checked-out-looking kid.)
Yes, but I'm feeling spacey. (Anxious, sad, mad, and then zoned out is Sheila's regular progression, and I imagine it was the progression of her infant self during the days in the hospital.)

Bounce that baby a little bit, very sweetly, so she knows you're there. Talk to her, the way you talked to your little sister.
Hi baby. I'm here. Mommy's here. Robin's here. It's okay now. You're not alone, anymore.

What happens for that inside baby when you connect to her?
She's less spacey, and I'm less spacey. And she's starting to get scared again.

Look into her eyes and let her know that you're here and I'm here and your mom's here . . . (Her shoulders, which had come up to her ears, slowly drop down.) *Are you always going to be around for that baby, even when you're older?*
Yes!

Cool. Then you better tell her that . . . Can you tell the mad baby, too? . . . And the scared baby . . . And the spaced out baby? (This kid is so dissociated that interventions don't generalize from one part to another.) *How are these little ones now?*
Better.

After several months Sheila came to sessions by herself and was most often in her presenting adolescent. She had some catching up to do, as she hadn't developed the self-soothing or affect-regulation skills of her age-mates. Much of our work was spent on skills to reduce effects of obsessive-compulsive disorder. I taught her to breathe deeply, ground herself, and examine the veracity of her fears. She became adept at identifying the age of the part of her that was distressed and settling it down. She started taking baby-sitting jobs, which gave her some competence to draw on.

I'm scared!

What of?
I have to go to the bathroom, and I'm afraid I'll be locked in (a fear she had when away from home).

What age is scared?
The three-year-old and the five-year-old.

Is there a baby-sitter part of you in the house?
Yeah.

Can the baby-sitter and the little ones come to the bathroom with me and check out its escapability?
Yes!
(Sheila and I get out of our chairs, walk into the small office bathroom, and discuss how to get out if locked in.)

Can a three-year-old open the door very well? Can a thirteen-year-old operate the door knob? Which part of you would be the right one to get in and out of this room? If the door got jammed shut for some reason, what would a baby-sitter do?
I'd yell for help, and you would come.

Right! What would you do if I didn't come?
I'd yell out the window. And then I'd wait to see if someone walked by and I'd yell again.

And if that didn't work, what would you do?
(She examines the door closely.) I'd try to take it off the hinges.

Brilliant. And how likely would it be that you'd have to do any of those things?
Not very likely.

Is it safe to go to the bathroom?
Yes!

When you're done, come back in the room, and we'll talk some more.

(After she returns from the bathroom:) *Sheila, what do you need to tell the three-year-old and the five-year-old?*

That they're safe with me and that I understand doors.

I think they get scared whenever there's a remote possibility that you could be separated from someone safe. Then they come up with another reason, like fear of a locked door, to keep you from doing things. Does that make sense?

Yes.

What do you need to tell them?

Little girls, I'm always here. I'm a baby-sitter and a big sister. I take care of kids all the time, and I know what to do. I won't let you get locked in, and you won't ever be alone, because I'm here.

This work allowed Sheila to function more like a person of her chronological age. She was doing well in school, was more independent, and was much happier. But there was an attachment piece still missing. Whenever a peer tried to get close to her, Sheila would push the person away. When her mother would hug her or reassure her, a part of Sheila would get angry or shut down completely. Therapists or parents might assume that she's an adolescent needing her independence. But that wasn't it.

Sheila's mother came in for two sessions, sitting close, making eye contact, and saying things like "I'm here. I love you. I want to connect with you." At these words, Sheila would immediately "switch" states and report to us, "I'm mad. I want to push you away . . . I'm getting a headache . . . I'm shutting down."

At the next session, Sheila was able to say that the part that gave her the headache was a baby part, a really strong one, and that the main problem was that it didn't want her to know that her mother existed. (*What a great defense!* I thought.)

Sheila, is that because if your mom existed, way back when, you might lose her again, and you couldn't stand it?
Yes!

Is that why that part of you gets so mad?
Yes!

What would happen to you if that baby part knew how much your mom has been there for you?
I don't know, but I'm getting spacey, and my head hurts.

We got "Almost Fifteen/Middle-School Graduate Girl" back into the room and tried to have her talk to the baby part, which only brought up more dissociative symptoms. Holding and talking to the baby didn't work. We tried a *Star Trek* "Vulcan mind-meld" between parts, to no avail. Finally my Milton Erickson–inspired brain that knew to use the client's own experience and metaphors figured out how to use the technology that this geeky girl knew the best.

Ms. Middle-School-Graduate Sheila, are you good at basic arithmetic?

Yeah, pretty good.

You're almost fifteen. How many days have you been alive, approximately? (I'll spare you the math discussions.)
Fifty-four hundred.

How many times has your mom hugged you in your life?
Eleven thousand.

How many times has she fed you?
At least twelve thousand.

How many times has she said, "I love you"?
Maybe five thousand.

How do you get music onto your iPod?
Download it from the computer.

How do you do that?
Plug in a cable and tell the computer to move the song over.

How long does it take?
A few seconds.

Did you know that the human brain downloads data hundreds of times faster than your computer?
Really? That's cool. (Keeping the conversation in a math and technology mode kept her most grown-up parts in the room. She reported no headaches and looked fully present in this conversation.)

Are you ready to download the data from your almost-fifteen-year-old to the headache part in the back of the brain?
Yeah. How will we do that?

Let's call up the headache part. Think about your mom gazing deeply into your eyes, loving you.
I'm getting a little spacey, and my head is hurting.

Put one hand right there, on that left brain where you have all the numbers and memories. Put the other one where your head is hurting . . . Good! That's your data cable. On the count of three, you will instantaneously download all the memory data of your mom loving you: eleven thousand hugs, twelve thousand meals, and five thousand I-love-yous to all your baby parts. Got it! Good! One, two, three! . . . Now take a deep breath and notice what happened.
(Sheila beams.) I feel happy.

Think about your mom looking into your eyes and loving you.
It makes me feel happy!

Look into my eyes, and notice what it's like to know that I've got the good kind of tears in them from feeling how good you feel now and knowing how hard it was for you before (Fosha, 2000). (This sort of thing used to trigger the same kind of spacing out and headache that her mom triggered.)
(Her eyes are shining.) I feel good and sad and happy.

Could you take my hands and keep looking at me and keep noticing what that's like?
It's good!

In subsequent sessions we found other dissociative parts, with different etiologies. One day Sheila reported, "I've been mad all day, and don't know why."

What's it about?
I don't know.

What age goes with that mad?
I don't know.

Where do you feel it?
In my arms.

Do you want to try pushing it out of your arms?
Yes!
(I move my chair closer to Sheila, while she puts her fists into my waiting palms. As she pushes my hands away, she begins to look fierce, then triumphant, then totally spaced out.)

What just happened?
My head hurts!

What part of you is making that happen?
Five.

What's happening from your five-year-old?
Don't be mad. Don't be sad.

Why not?

Because Daddy will lock the door. (On further exploration, Sheila told me that her father would lock her in her bedroom when she got "too sad or too mad." I imagine that it was when her out of control infant states would arise.)

Does this explain your fear of locked bathroom doors?
Yes!

So you were able to control the too sad and too mad by spacing out?
(She nods.)
   And the headaches were to warn you when you started feeling a lot? (She nods.)
   I'm going to ask some stupid therapy questions for your almost-fifteen-year-old: Is it okay to cry or feel angry, now?
Yes.

Are you appropriate with those feelings, like not being weird around people your age?
Yes.

Do you still live with your father?
No.

Does anyone ever lock you in a room now?
No.

And could you get out, if they tried?
Yes!
(I'm front-loading the intervention.)

Okay, then! Let's liberate these younger parts of you. Ms. Nearly Fifteen, let's fly down to the youngest age you ever got locked in your room. How old were you?

Four.

Unlock that door. Go into that room, and introduce yourself to that little one. Tell her that you're getting her out of that room, forever . . . Now pick her up. Got her? Carry her out of that door and out of the house, and walk her over to where you live now, with your mother. Let her feel how high up she is in your arms; you're almost grown-up size. Let her see where you live. Let her know that nobody ever locks you in. And that you understand locks, now . . . What do I mean? Show her your keys. Show her every time you've ever unlocked a front door, or a bathroom door, or a combination lock at school or on your bike. And let her know that she never, ever has to go back to that room. What percent of that four-year-old do we have out of that room?

She's still scared.

Let's go get her again. Let's get all the locked-in ages. When did it stop?

When I was six.

Okay. Ready? Ms. Nearly Fifteen, let's go back to the four-year-old, the first time she got locked in. Unlock that door, pick her up again, and this time bring all the ages of all the times it happened, four years old, five years old, six years old . . . Do you have them all? Your arms must be really full! Then fly them up the years: seven, eight, nine, ten, eleven, twelve, thirteen, fourteen, to almost fifteen. Are there any left back there? Let's do one more

sweep. Start at four, the first time you got locked in: four, five, six,
seven, eight, nine, ten, eleven, twelve, thirteen, fourteen, almost
fifteen   Show those kids around again to this time, right now
(Paul, 2007)
(Sheila is grinning, shoulders unhunched, breathing deeply.)
I feel good.
(We talk for a while. She is relaxed and almost giddy with
relief. I am a little afraid to test the integration, but I want to
make sure that Sheila is all here and all now.)

Let's see if it's okay, inside, to be mad. Think of something that
makes you mad. Your sister being a brat? Good choice. Where do
you feel that? Your arms? I see that you have fists. Put those fists
into my palms and push, slowly, slowly, but harder.
(Sheila, looking angry, pushes my hands all the way back as
she strongly extends her arms. At the end of the extension
she's smiling and takes a deep breath.)

What's that like?
Good!!

Is it safe to be mad or sad?
Yes!

Do you stay mad forever?
No. It can go away, now, because I feel it.

That's brilliant! Lots of adults don't know that. Are there times, you
being a cool teenager, that you will choose not to show all your emotions?

Yes! (laughing).

But it's okay to have them anyway?
Yes!

As Sheila continued to integrate her dissociated parts, she became more and more mature. Even though she was a constitutionally anxious kid, she grew in confidence and healthy self-awareness. She was able to report about how she handled younger parts coming forward. On the first day of high school, she told me: "I was scared, and I didn't want to talk to anyone. I wanted my mom. Then I remembered that I was fifteen and I was okay. This girl talked to me at lunch, and I started to get spacey. I told my three-year-old that it was okay, and that I could talk, and that it was safe. Then I had fun talking to the girl. She's in my English class. We might be friends, later." (Formerly, younger parts had blocked friendships, on the premise that attachment meant loss.)

WRAPPING UP

Because most persistent ego states arise in childhood, most ego state work makes bridges between the oldest, most competent part of the client and child states. The more you do this work, the more you will notice child states arising in your clients. Most interventions in this book involve connecting child states to resourced adult states.

Part II

PROBLEM-SPECIFIC INTERVENTIONS

CHAPTER 5

Working With Trauma

After we have been in real or perceived danger, our brains play the scenario over and over. Simple, single-event traumas can replay as the image of what happened and the emotions and body sensations of the event. After trauma, our brains may put our bodies on red alert status at any reminder of the traumatic event. Even though the thinking front parts of our brain know that we survived that car accident, assault, or tongue lashing, the amygdala and hippocampus in the back brain can put us into a vigilant, flight-or-fight state.

If the trauma was relatively recent, was singular, and was experienced by a person not prone to dissociation, the "parts" are imaginal. When the trauma happened early in life, was repetitive, or was perpetrated by a trusted caregiver, it may create deep neural pathways of existence, defenses, and behavior: dissociated ego states with state-specific beliefs, including "the world is unsafe," "people aren't to be trusted," and "I'm not worthy of being safe, protected, or loved."

Ego state therapy is one of many ways to treat trauma. EMDR, somatic therapies, exposure therapies, the counting method, and many more modalities can clear simple trauma. Ego state therapy, with its inherent creation of a dual attention (the trauma vs. right now), can move simple trauma and is a necessary component of work with complex trauma. Several EMDR books address using ego state therapy, blending the neurological component of EMDR's bilateral stimulation with the dual attention of different states. I often combine ego state work with EMDR and with relational therapies, such as CIMBS, complex integration of multiple brain systems (Sheldon & Sheldon, 2010), and accelerated experiential dynamic psychotherapy (Fosha, 2000). Traumatized people can be complicated. I hope you find the following trauma protocols helpful and then learn several more modalities so that you have many tools to use with this population.

SIMPLE TRAUMA

1. Solidify the here-and-now part of your clients' strengths by having them imagine a role or an activity in which they have felt strong, competent, protective, or nurturing—whatever is needed (Korn & Leeds, 2002).

2. Have the here-and-now part identify the part that is stuck in the trauma.

3. Have the here-and-now part reach into the past, grab hold of the willing traumatized part, and pull it into the present time and place.

4. Have the present part orient the past part to the present safety.

5. Check back for leftover trauma. Pull through again, until the trauma is done.

6. Hug the younger part inside.

This technique includes some EMDR-based resource installation (Leeds, 2009), some life span integration (Pace, 2007), time travel, and some of my own modifications to each.

CASE EXAMPLE PTSD From a Single Trauma

John, 24, went to the local swimming hole one hot summer night. It was dark. He and his friends were drinking. After a deep dive off the log raft, John became disoriented. At first he panicked, looking wildly around, searching for "up," but the cloudy sky was as dark as the lake bottom. For a few long minutes he thrashed around, until he gave up and went limp. His heart pounding loudly in his ears, he slowly floated to the surface, not knowing until he reached it that he would live and breathe again.

After the accident, John had classic symptoms of PTSD: nightmares of drowning in the dark, an aversion to taking showers or baths, an aversion to alcohol, an exaggerated startle response, more worry, a quicker temper, and a sense of hopelessness. After three weeks of nightmares, he was avoiding going to bed. During a ninety-minute session, I started with an assessment: good family, good attachment, few traumas, not addicted to anything, a normal guy with PTSD. I asked John to think of a time when he felt strong and in control. He thought about working out with weights at the gym. I asked him if he ever had opportunities to help people. Again, his mind went to the gym, "spotting" for other guys when they lifted weights.

First we accessed his strong, helpful gym-rat presence:

John think about spotting for someone at the gym. Can you feel the strength in your body? Your state of being alert and relaxed at the same time? Your care for the other person? Good. Hold onto this state. Now think about that night, being underwater in that lake. Reach out from right here and right now and grab that drowning guy by the arms. Pull him through the last three weeks to right here and right now. (Now hand him a towel, he's dripping all over my office!) *Tell that guy a few things. One, tell him that he didn't drown. Two, tell him that it's over. Three, take some deep breaths, right now. Are you breathing water or air?*
Air

If it's air and you're here, did you survive?
Yes.

You've got him here. Show him around. Does he know he survived?
Finally. (He sighs and relaxes.)

Okay. Think back to being under the water, not knowing which way is up . . . What do you notice now?
Better, but still scary.

Get ready to reach back there again. Are you grounded in the now? Are you strong? Reach back, grab him, and pull that part of you up here.
(John goes through the movement again, completes it, and sighs again.) I think I got him all here.

Good job! What's it feel like?

I feel like I've relaxed for the first time since that night.

Great! Think about the lake. Imagine jumping into it in the daytime, sober.
No sweat.

Imagine curling up in bed at night and falling asleep.
Sounds good!

Is there anything left over?
Yeah, I shouldn't jump into dark water in the middle of the night . . . especially not when I'm high.

Well, yeah! Do you have a sense of your slightly younger, wetter self still here.
A little.

Take him by the arms again, pull him toward you, and as you pull, let him melt back into you.
Okay.

How does that feel?
Good.

Think about that dark night again.
There's nothing there to think about. It happened.

Great!

REPETITIVE TRAUMA THAT IS NO LONGER OCCURRING

1. The clients identify what happened, how many times, and the time frame of events.
2. Solidify the here-and-now part of your clients' strengths by having them imagine a role or an activity in which they feel strong, competent, protective, or nurturing—whatever is needed.
3. Have the here-and-now part identify the part that is stuck in the trauma.
4. Find a label or name with which to refer to the traumatized part. You may want to refer to the feeling state that goes with the trauma: scared kid, shamed little girl, shut-down boy, angry teenager, and so forth.
5. Have the here-and-now part reach into the past to the first time the event occurred, grab hold of the willing traumatized part, and pull that traumatized part into the present time and place.
6. Have the present part orient the past part to the present safety. "Is your angry dad still alive?" "Do you still live on that block with that bully?" "Are you out of that middle school?" *Tell your "younger self" that it's over and he lives here with you now.*
7. Have clients go back to that first instance. Have the resourced adult part sweep up all the younger ages, through all the years, that are still stuck in the trauma, all the way up to now. This may be in the form of one ever-growing child or the sense of an armload of children (a modification of Pace, 2007).

8. Orient the child parts to the present safety and present life.
9. Check back for leftover trauma. Pull through again, until the trauma is done.
10. Hug the younger part(s) inside.

CASE EXAMPLE **EMDR for Repetitive Trauma**

Mary, forty-five, had an extremely controlling and abusive father and a meek mother and had learned to submit to and placate everyone around her. She had some dissociation but did not have DID. We had used a mixture of EMDR and the simple trauma protocol to clear out the worst traumas in her life, including sexual assaults, a horrible car accident, and particularly bad physical and emotional abuse. In third grade she had moved from the city to a farm, far outside a small town. A shy girl and an outsider, she had been bullied from the day she had started school until she graduated from high school. As a result, she was anxious, tentative in most social situations, unassertive, and sure that people would not like her. We had successfully used EMDR on the worst bullying incidents, but the issue had failed to completely clear, and we moved to ego state therapy.

Mary, let's find your strongest, most protective part.
I don't know what that is (apologetically).

Imagine you're out walking with your daughter, and someone tries to attack her.
I'd kill them.

That works for me! Notice your posture and your clenched fists.

Notice the protectiveness you're feeling in your body. Do you feel like a full-grown adult? (She nods emphatically.) *Ready to go protect that girl you used to be?* (She raises her fists like a boxer.) *Let's go! Go back to the first days of school; see that shy, adorable little girl you were. Did she deserve to be bullied?*
No.

Did she deserve to be protected?
Yes, all children should be protected.

What should have happened in that school?
The kids should have been instructed how to treat a new student.

What else should have happened?
The minute the bullying started, the teacher or some other adults should have intervened.

I'm glad you know that! So find that third-grader. The moment the bullying starts, I want you to sweep her up and out of there and tell her what you just told me . . . How is she taking your information?
Relief.

Start sweeping her up through the years, bringing up every age of girl from that school until you get her completely away from those mean kids . . . With your arms full of girls, fly her through the decades until you get right here and right now in my office. Is it one girl or a lot of girls.
Many ages.

Do they all fit on that couch with you?
Yes, somehow.

Let them know where they are. (Notice the talking through the adult to the parts.) *Are all the parts of you safe here?*
Yes.

Do they know it?
(She pauses.) A little.

Your grown-up protective part needs to let them know that they're safe here. No bullies in this room! . . . Let them know what you knew about that town and that school: that you didn't deserve to be bullied and that you should have been protected. Make sure every age of you knows that.
(Mary is silent for a few minutes, her eyes moving from place to place near her.) I did it, and they all know.

What are you feeling now?
They're sad, and I'm sad. (Notice the switch from fear to sadness, a normal progression in most trauma therapies.)

Let's hang out with sadness for a while. Let those kid parts know that it's good to be sad about a sad thing that happened . . . (Mary looks down, and then looks up again.) *Show those kids where you live now. Show them your sweet husband, and your still-young-enough-to-be-sweet daughter. Introduce them to your sweet dog . . . Your good friends . . . Your reasonably nice boss . . . And your fantastic therapist.* (Mary laughs.)

Does anybody bully you now?
No.

Is your life reasonably safe?
Yes.

Do these kids know it?
(She looks around.) Yes.

Try something: Ask these parts if it's safe to come inside into one body.
(Mary considers for a moment.) Yes.

Physically pull them together into one girl. (I stretch my arms wide and pull them together to show her. She does the same.) *Hug her to you.* (She does.) *Let that little girl know that she never, ever has to go back to that school and be a kid and be abused by anyone . . .*
She knows!

And when you're ready, hug her into you. (She does, with a big sigh.)

How does it feel?
Good and different.

How so?
I feel like a grown-up. In fact, I know I'm okay, and that I'm an adult, for the first time.

Wonderful! Stay with that for a moment . . . What happens when you think of the bullying?

It feels like a long time ago and that it's over.

What happens when you think of going to a party?
I feel a little nervous, but not like before . . . I can handle it.

And what happens when you think of that coworker who takes credit for all your good work.
(She makes fists.) I'll set the record straight.

As you go through the week, notice how you are reacting in social situations. Notice what's different, and notice if any of your bullied kid arises. If she does, do you know how to take care of her now?
I'll talk to her and let her know that I'm taking care of things and hug her back inside.

You've got it!

SUMMING UP TRAUMA

While ego state work is one of many trauma therapies, it can be used with all levels of trauma, from the most simple, one-time event to the most complex, attachment-disordered, repeatedly traumatic experiences. Ego state therapy is essential for clients with complex dissociation and can be integrated with many other therapies or used as the main therapy for these cases. (See Chapter 8 for a case example of working with a suicidal DID client.)

CHAPTER 6

Working With Relationship Challenges

People bring their attachment histories into every relationship. Babies form bonds with the people and beings around them, building a separate neural network with its own set of responses for each caregiver, family member, creature, and many inanimate objects (dolls, blankies, pacifiers.) When early attachment goes well, children learn to expect kindness, consistency, and good attention from other people. When consistently responded to, children grow their own capacities for self-soothing, tolerating feelings, and knowing that they are important and worth the good treatment that they receive (Schore, 1994; Siegel, 1999). When children are inconsistently responded to, abused, or neglected or have "scary" depressed, angry, addicted, or disso-ciated parents, their brains grow neural pathways for interacting with those kinds of people. Louis Cozolino (2006) says that kids that have scary parents develop reflexive opiate responses to abu-sive people, thus experiencing a comforting rush of good feeling around people who are inadequate, spaced out, or abusive like the folks at home. (This explains how an otherwise sane person can pick horrible partner after horrible partner.) With ego state work, we can identify the young parts that are attracted to jerks, or the teenage parts that don't want to be told what to do, while we identify and authorize wiser adult parts to take over the choices and functions of adult relationships.

Finding the adult part that can avoid an inappropriate partner and find a good partner

1. Engage the oldest, wisest adult part by calling on professional expertise, parenting, or other adult states.

2. Find the troubled child part by connecting with the part that keeps falling for inappropriate partners.

3. Bring the child part to the adult's lap.

4. Point out how that child/infant is yearning for and reaching out toward that inappropriate person.

5. Turn the child toward the adult.

6. Have the adult speak to the child, while looking into its eyes, holding it around the shoulders, feeling its weight on the adult's knees, saying

   a. I'm your adult.

   b. I'm always here for you, all day and all night.

   c. I'm the one that can hold you when you're lonely or upset.

   d. I'm the one that takes care of you.

   e. I'm the one who will never, ever leave." (I point out that the adult can't leave because the adult and child are "stuck together.")

   f. "And I'm the grown-up. I'm the one who is old enough to

pick the person that we can love and that has the ability to love us back. It's a grown-up job.

    g. I'll listen to what you want, but I'll make my grown-up decisions about it."

7.   Ask how the child part feels (often some relief and some sadness) and how the adult part feels (usually strong).

8.   Have the adult hug the child back inside, feeling it as the child part of the whole person. *Where does that child part live inside of you? How can you comfort it, when you're making grown-up decisions?*

9.   Have the client imagine meeting and sparking with a potential dysfunctional partner. Have the client imagine sweeping the child part behind, saying "I'll handle this," and running away.

10.   Have the client imagine meeting a nice, sane, attractive person. Tell the client: *You won't feel the initial arousal with this person, because you're not sensing danger and feeling the fear that you've always confused with excitement. And you won't feel that flood of well-being that comes with all those opiates rising in you to handle the fear. Imagine how you would assess that person with your most adult brain . . . Imagine how you would interact with that person from your adult part. What are you feeling right now?*

CASE EXAMPLE Disengaging From an Inappropriate Partner

Jane is a thirty-three-year-old professional with emotionally abusive parents and a history of relationships with needy, seductive, abusive men. She is considering breaking up with Tim, her latest guy, who clearly has borderline personality disorder, alternately whining, threatening suicide, solicitous, and raging. We had done the two-hand technique about Tim:

Hold the part of you that yearns for Tim and feels that she can't live without him in one hand. Hold the part of you that is afraid of Tim, angry at him, and is ready to get away from the drama in the other hand. What do you notice? (She notices that her hands feel very different.)

Feel the one who is ready to run. How old is she?
Lots of ages, but mostly adult.

Find the most adult part of her. What do you see through her eyes?
I see a guy who is a mess, and a woman acting like a little kid.

Can you feel that kid's hand? How old is that little kid?
She's somewhere between a baby and about four.

Can you feel her reaching out toward that crazy guy? (She nods.)
    Pick her up, put her on your lap, and turn that little girl to face you. (Jane makes the motions.)
    Put your hands around her back to support her. Feel the weight of that child's body on your lap. Let her feel your strong arms around her and your strong legs holding her up. Look her straight in the eye and see that beautiful, yearning child. Let her see you as you are most adult, able to connect with her. Can you see her and feel her? (She nods.) *Can she see and feel you?* (She nods. We've established the necessary dual attention, with techniques borrowed from Steele [2007a].)

It's time for that most adult part of you to explain what's happening. When you've told that little girl each of these things, give me a nod or a signal that you've told her and she understands. "I'm your adult. I'm always here for you, all day and all night. I'm the one that can hold you when you're lonely or upset. I'm the one that takes care of you. I'm the one who will never, ever leave, because you live inside of me. I can't go anywhere without you. You will never be alone again." . . .

Jane, will you be responsible for feeding this child good food, every day? Will you make sure she gets enough rest? Will you make sure that both your adult and kid parts have time off to play? Will you keep you and this child safe? Will you protect this kid part of you from scary, dangerous people? I don't want to have to call Child Protective Services. (This joke, which I borrow from Stephen Gilligan, always makes people laugh and commit to avoiding dangerous situations.)

Are you ready to tell that child part that you're taking over your love life? Here is one way: Tell her "I'm the grown-up. I'm the one who is old enough to pick the person that we can love and that has the ability to love us back. It's a grown-up job . . . I'm keeping us away from abusive people, including Tim, even if it makes you sad, because I'm taking care of you. It's okay to be sad. I'll help you. I'm here." (Often times, the client has been avoiding the grief of leaving because younger parts don't have the affect tolerance to move through the grief.)

Jane, what are you feeling right now?
The little one is frantic and I'm telling her that I'm here with her . . . She's settling down now to just sad. I'm sad, but I can deal with it. (Jane leaks tears, looking present and contained.)

Stay with that for a while.

What do you notice, now?
I can handle it. I can be sad. I just have to hold onto my little girl. (She sighs.)

Let's think of some other times it would be good to hold onto that little girl. Think about the next time Tim calls. He's going be to really nice, trying to get you to come back.
My little girl just perked up. She's ready to go back.

What's your adult think about this?
Bad idea!

Can you sweep that little girl behind you? (I sweep my hand from front to back, as if I'm pushing a child back behind me in a protective way.) *Tell her that this is grown-up stuff and you'll handle it.*
(Jane sweeps her arm back.) Get back there! He's dangerous. I'll handle this.

Now imagine dealing with Tim from your adult.
It feels good. I feel strong. And I'm not getting hooked.

Great! Now imagine being home alone and lonely and thinking of calling Tim. What do you do?
I need to connect to this little one and let her know I'm here.

Great! Imagine doing that . . . How does it work?
Well, but I can still feel that lonely feeling.

Of course you do. Try this: Imagine all the people that love you, where it hasn't gone wrong. How many do you have?
Five.

Put them in an arc in front of you, look into their eyes, and get a dose of their love right through your eyes to your heart. Or from their hearts to yours and your heart to theirs. Try it both ways and see which works better for you . . . Who in this group is around here and should be on your schedule? It will help you and your little girl to know when you get to see the people that support you. Imagine setting up regular dates with people. Imagine having regular phone calls or Skyping with the people who are out of town. (If you do EMDR, this would be a great time for some bilateral stimulation.)
I'd still miss Tim, but it would feel good to know when I get to be with my friends or talk to my grandma.

When it's the middle of the night or another time when you feel lonely and can't connect with anyone, you can imagine your circle of love and keep sending that love back and forth, heart to heart. Imagine that again.
Still feels great.

It's the end of the session. Are you ready to bring that little girl back inside of you?
Yes!

So hug her close, and hug her in. Let me know when she's all the way inside . . . Where does she live inside of you, now?
In my heart.

Of course! Can you check in on her at least once a day, until we meet again?

I'd be glad to!

In the next session, Jane told me that when Tim called she'd felt strongly adult and had reiterated her boundaries with him: no more calling, no dates, no booty calls. He got weepy and obsequious on the phone. First she felt sad for him, and when she began to feel "young" and guilty she identified the little girl. "I swept her back behind me, saying 'I'll handle this,' and I told Tim that I needed to go. He got really mad and called me a bitch. I told him that that wouldn't work anymore and turned off my phone for an hour. I had tons of messages from him and I just deleted them. I feel a little sad and very relieved. My little girl feels a little sad and glad to be with me, because I'm nicer and always there. And it's weird, she's starting to fade. I'm not feeling her as much, anywhere in my life."

FINDING AN APPROPRIATE PARTNER

A few sessions later, we worked on how to pick a good boyfriend. After discussing how to find a nice guy, we made a list of the attributes she wanted in a guy: sane, nice, safe, attractive, shared values, respectful, good communicator, connectible, ambitious, and grown-up. And we made a second list of what she didn't want: crazy, dangerous, addicted, mean, manipulative, too needy, deadbeat, and stupid. We first imagined that she met a cute guy with a mean, manipulative streak.

Imagine you meet a really attractive man. He's very nice and a

little overinterested. You start getting really excited. That old rush comes over you. What do you do now?
I'm ready to jump on him, right now!

Try this: find that kid part of you, and sweep her back behind you. "I'll deal with this!" Then start to assess this guy with your adult brain. What do you look for?
I'll ask him about other relationships. If all the women were "bitches," then I know he's a jerk. If I pull back a little, or put him off, I'll watch how he deals with it. And I'll see how he treats other people.

What do you do if he insists?
Just say <u>NO</u>! I'll tell him that I'm not interested and to back off.

A bit later in the session, I ask her to think about meeting a guy who fits her want list criteria but with whom she doesn't have that initial response of fear and arousal confused with sexual arousal.

Part of me wants to just walk away.

Which part is that?
My seventeen-year-old. She's bored with him.

What do you need to do about that?
(She sighs.) Tell her that she doesn't get to pick them any-more, since she always picks crazy jerks . . . They're exciting, but I'm done with them . . . So I tell her, "Get thee behind me! I'm going to check this guy out and see if we might actu-

ally like him." (She sweeps her hand from front to back.) You know, he's kind of cute. (She giggles.)

Here's your assignment. I want you to check out every guy you come across, married, single, gay, straight, or whatever, and see which ones fit your adult criteria. Now, don't hit on them. This is just practice using your new criteria. Check out characters on TV, in the movies, and in books. Train your brain to have a new filter. And don't forget to have fun doing it! Could this be fun?
Yeah, and I can see bringing my girlfriends into the evaluation process. This could be even more fun.

(EMDR note: You can use this practice as a future template.)

BEING AN ADULT IN A RELATIONSHIP

People need their adult brains engaged in order to find good partners. After finding partners, they need even more adult presence in order to have a good relationship. In functional, happy relationships, partners easily slide between states. Partners may activate the happy kids in one another; be in a nurturing, parental adult state when the other one is in sick or sad "kid" mode; and go into full-on intellectual mode to deal with finances or pick good schools for the kids.

Even the healthiest relationships have times of inappropriate states. Think of the last time you had a conflict with your partner. Did you stay in your calm, collected, problem-solving adult state or become a tantrum-throwing two-year-old? Did you jump to your judgmental parental part or your acting-out, "you can't make me do that" teenager? I haven't met anyone, so far, who is always in functional adult during conflict.

Problems arise when partners get stuck in habitual, dysfunctional roles, emotional states, or "parts" with each other. Sometimes these ego states are created during the relationship. Often, they are reactivated states from childhood or earlier relationships. Parts can become reciprocal: he goes into his incompetent, passive-aggressive kid, while she becomes the rage-filled avenger (with a scared little girl inside). She regresses to the terrified, obedient child state that barely survived her childhood when he regresses to his three-year-old overly entitled pissed-off toddler state or his angry teenager. The permutations are endless. The therapeutic goal is to promote adult states that are capable of reason, intimacy, decent boundaries, and love, that can carry on the tasks of adult relationship, and that can contain their own dysfunctional younger parts.

The tasks of adult relationships include

⫶ David Schnarch's (1997) "holding onto yourself," being able to self-soothe during conflict;

⫶ seeing your partner in a realistic way: not expecting partners to meet your every need;

⫶ knowing how to take care of yourself when your partner can't or won't;

⫶ differentiating your partner from your parents or other past relationships

⫶ differentiating yourself from your partner, and being okay with that—knowing it's safe (and inevitable) to be different (Schnarch calls this tolerating the anxiety of being different);

||| holding an ambivalent object—loving your partner, even when angry or disappointed, being able to hold your partner as a mix of the good stuff and the other stuff;

||| being able to engage the playful child in both of you when appropriate and the wise adults when necessary;

||| in conflict, being able to hold both your own and your partner's needs and opinions as valid, while working toward a solution;

||| being able to set firm limits on an abusive or dangerous partner or an issue about which you feel strongly; and

||| understanding that your partner's reactions are "not about me" (Bader & Pearson, 1988).

If your client never witnessed or took part in a healthy relationship, you need to do some psychoeducation about these tasks. Books, a good couples' workshop (e.g., Bader & Pearson, 1988; Gottman & Silver, 1999), or working through the above list can be helpful. However, information is not enough to keep a well-informed client from traveling well-worn neural highways into habitual dysfunction. Both partners triggering each other can lead to a familiar folie à deux, both reprising their favored old (young) dysfunctional roles.

Finding and staying in adult

1. Engage the oldest, wisest adult part by calling on professional expertise, parenting, or other adult states. The best way, if possible, is to find the adult part that has been wise, patient, and understanding with the partner.

2. Find the child part that has been too present in the relationship.

3. "Talk through" the adult part to the child:
   a. How old is this part?
   b. What does this part need? (Common needs include safety, feeling seen, not being seen as bad.)
   c. Have the adult part meet these needs ("you're safe with me," "I see you and you're my favorite kid," "I know you're a good kid").
   d. The adult hugs the child back inside.
4. Imagine scenarios that brought up that child part and have the client imagine saying, "I'll deal with this!" and sweeping the child behind in order to face the partner as an adult.
5. If the client is involved with a habitually angry, abusive, or not very grown-up partner, teach the client to consciously notice and respond to the state shifts in the partner (J. Golston, personal communication, 2003). It takes adult consciousness to notice these things. If the client is in an adult state, the situation is much less likely to turn ugly. This is a great time for an adult part to sweep the child part behind, assess the situation, and take charge.
6. Imagine habitual dysfunctional scenarios, bringing the adult forward to care for and protect the child and interact with the partner. This may happen in one session or many, depending on the client and the relationship.

CASE EXAMPLE **Containing Anxiety and Anger in Fears of Merging**

Larry, forty-two, had dated but had never been in a long-term relationship. His goal in therapy was to be able to "get along with women." He was attractive and intelligent and worked in the tech industry. Unlike some in that industry, he had no trace of autistic behavior. His history was "normal," but he had trouble being open for about most of his childhood. I could tell that he was wary of me and unusually specific about his boundaries for scheduling and the length of the therapy. I watched him carefully as I pushed him for more specifics. He finally admitted that his mother had been "too" present, to the point of intrusiveness, and that she was reactive to his every response and action. As a result he was defensive and fearful of disclosing, and in relationships was often dumped for his lack of emotional availability.

Much of the therapy played out in the transference. When I would ask Larry about any internal process, he would reflexively push back, saying "What's it to you?" or "Why do you want to know?" or by sitting and glaring at me. After a few sessions of carefully explaining everything, I changed my tactics.

> *Larry, I'm going to ask you to do something really weird and probably really uncomfortable, and I'd like you, just for a while, to answer all my questions, without question, and do exactly what I tell you. I invite you to feel everything you feel and to use those feelings to answer the questions. If it becomes too much, raise your hand or say "Too much!" and we'll stop. Can you agree with this?* (Larry ponders for half a minute and then nods, looking intrigued.)
>
> *First, I'd like you to get in touch with that smart guy in you, the one who writes and analyzes software and who interacts well with the guys at work . . . Found him?* (He nods.) *I want to ask that part of you the questions, and get the answers through him.* (He nods again.) *Okay, Mr. Tech, could you do a search inside Larry and tell me which age or ages get up in arms when I ask a question?*

Fourteen to eighteen.

And what ages is that teenager protecting?
(Larry ponders for a few minutes, thinking hard.) Many ages
. . . Very young to right now.

What is that teenager protecting all the ages of you from?
Disappearing . . . Wow!

Explain "wow."
If she was there, I couldn't be there. (He shivers.)

*If your mother was present, you couldn't be there? Say more about
that.*
I don't know . . . She was so scared. There wasn't room for me
to know anything about myself, if I was paying attention to
her. So after a while I cut her off.

I was starting to see that this guy was a classic "drama of the
gifted child" person (Miller, 1981), with a huge defensive over-
lay. I explained my theory, that he was projecting his overwhelming mom on every woman, including me, and reflexively
trying to protect his kid parts from annihilation. Larry nodded
throughout the explanation.

You got me. What do I do now? This stuff is wrecking my
relationships.

*We have a lot to do. That teenage defensive part of you is the most
obvious target, but that overwhelmed little boy part of you needs*

to know he's safe, that he doesn't have to take care of anyone, and to know that you are taking care of him. In the meantime, your valiant defender can have a much deserved vacation, until he's reassigned by your most adult part. What does Mr. Tech think of the plan? Any questions?

It's interesting. How does the vacation work?

Can I show you? (He nods.) I need your most grown-up parts. Your tech guy, we have. We need a part of you that knows how to nurture, without disappearing and with having boundaries. Have you ever, as an adult, taken care of someone, where it worked out well for both of you?

Larry told me about helping a friend who had badly broken his leg while skiing. He'd brought food, helped him to the bathroom, and taken him to some appointments. He'd felt okay saying "no" to some requests, because other caregivers were involved. He'd felt good about helping, not overwhelmed.

Great! Where does that helpful, boundaried part of you live in your body? (Larry thumps his chest.) And where does your tech guy live? (Larry points to his head.) Feel both of them in your body and notice when you've used them both together . . . Got it? (He nods.) Imagine traveling back in time to when you were fourteen years old. Introduce yourself, so that he doesn't think you're a creep. Ask him to accompany you up through the years, bringing all ages of teenager, fourteen, fifteen, sixteen, seventeen, eighteen, nineteen, and all the way up to twenty (a variation on life span integration [Pace, 2007]). Bring that teenager up to now and show him around. Show him your fancy condo and that muscle car you drive. Show him where you work and your paycheck. Show him something particularly brilliant that you've done at work. What's he think?

He's totally awed.

Now show him how you took care of your friend, without disappearing . . . And show him you, as your adult, saying "no" about something at work. And show him how you say "no" to your mother, sometimes, from your not-so-reactive adult. (He nods.) *Can that kid part of you see that you can be nurturing?* (He nods.) *Smart?* (He nods.) *Have boundaries?*

Yup.

Where in your body does he know that? (He puts his hands on his chest and belly.) *Does that teenage kid feel safe with leaving the protection job up to your smart, nurturing, boundaried adult parts?*

Yeah.

And do those adult parts pledge to protect all ages of you, by having good boundaries and standing up, in an adult way, to mom and anyone else who might overwhelm you? (He nods.) *And to nurture that little kid inside you, that we haven't got to yet?* (He nods, looking much softer.) *So how is that teenager, now?*

He's relieved. He's lighter. And he's not so mad.

Great! Can you have your adult ask that kid when he might have fun being around your life? The operative word here is "fun," because this kid hasn't had enough.

(He thinks for a bit.) When I play video games, when I'm

eating ribs because we love ribs, and when I'm learning something really cool, he can be around.

And it's your adult that decides when you're done with the game or have had enough ribs?
Okay. (He sighs.)

Can you hug that teenager back inside of you?
(He wraps his arms around himself and squeezes.) Done.

In the next session, Larry was much more relaxed, less suspicious, and easier to engage. First we checked in on the teenage part, which was barely there. Then we did a standard scenario of the adult taking care of the small inner child. Part of the message to the child was that he was good, even if his mother or other people around were having feelings or being nervous, and that the adult would assess the situation to see if the adult needed to take care of anything.

We imagined several adult scenarios, including Larry noticing his mother's anxiety, being kind to her, and setting appropriate limits; Larry interacting with one of his former girlfriends, "a nice one," using his kind and boundaried adult persona; and using his smart software analyst self to assess new girlfriend candidates for a good fit. Larry was sad and regretful in this process, saying, "I really blew it with lots of people. I didn't know how to defend myself any other way. Damn, that sucks." I supported him to stay with the feelings. He cried a bit and then looked up at me and said, "I didn't know how else to do it, until now . . . I can do it differently, if I remember to be adult around people." We discussed several scenarios that might bring the overwhelmed child and the defending teenager back and imagined containing the little one and sweeping back the teen. "I know what to do, now."

I saw Larry for several more sessions. Nearly a year later, he e-mailed me that he was in a relationship "with a good one" and was thinking of proposing. He said that he explained his teenage part to his girlfriend, who would say, "I want a real man to argue with, not a kid!" when the obnoxious part of him came out, which was increasingly rare.

CASE EXAMPLE Finding Adults in Two Partners

Mona, thirty-five, and Mary, thirty-seven, had been together for ten years. Mona was gregarious, outspoken, and sometimes explosive. Mary was introverted, a highly sensitive person (Aron, 1996), and cowed by Mona's anger. In the intake, we had noted the difference in personality and culture. Mona, a teacher, was Jewish, a second-generation immigrant, and from a big city. Mary, a copy editor, was from a rural community with a quiet, conflict-averse Protestant background. They had complementary complaints: Mona wanted Mary to "step up and show up" and express more of what she wanted and to "stop hiding from me all the time." She wanted more engagement. Mary wanted Mona to give her more space, stop nagging, and stop blowing up. Both wanted to feel closer. Both wanted to want (Schnarch, 1997) to have sex more often. I asked them the Bader and Pearson (1988) question, "What would you like to change in yourself to help the relationship?" Mona wanted to be able to "back off and to listen better." Mary wanted to "be able to stand up to Mona" and to tolerate Mona's big feelings.

After psychoeducation about differentiation and the warning by

Gottman and Silver (1999) that 69 percent of conflict in relationships is repetitive and never "solved" but merely tolerated, we started the ~~work. With both partners present, we started with Mona.~~

When Mary goes into the other room and gets quiet, what happens inside of you?
I get mad.

Take a minute and go inside. Is there a feeling underneath the anger?
I get scared.

What's that fear about?
I'm losing her. (Mona's voice gets soft and high, betraying a younger part.)

Is there an age that goes with that?
Lots of ages . . . It's tied to my mom getting mad and screaming and walking out on me or my dad. She'd get really mad and yell, and then leave. She'd shut herself into the bedroom or leave the house . . . I remember waiting for hours for her to open the door. When she left the house, I didn't know if she would ever come back. I'd stand by the window and watch for her car.

Did that little girl have other feelings?
She thought it was her fault. She felt ashamed.

Do you think it was her fault?
No. My mom was sort of crazy.

First a stupid therapy question: Did your mom always come back? (Mona nods.) She always did, anywhere from ten minutes to a couple of hours later.

Good! I want you to think of yourself at work, standing in front of the class, in charge and doing a great job teaching. Got it? . . . So can your competent grown-up go back to that time when you lived at home and your mom kept leaving you? . . . Can you find that kid back there and pull her aside? How's she feeling? Curious.

Now introduce yourself, so she doesn't think you're some creep. (Mona laughs and nods.) *Tell that kid a few things. Number one: Mom always, always came back. Number two: It wasn't her fault that Mom was yelling. Mom is a yelling kind of person, no matter what you did. Number three: It wasn't her fault that Mom would slam out.* (Notice that I had front-loaded the information from the competent adult part before floating back to the child.) *Number four, and best of all: This child has you now, and you can't leave her and won't leave her. Show her that you're an expert with kids. Have you ever slammed out of your classroom, abandoning your kids?* No, but I've thought about it a few times.

Why didn't you do it? Because I'm an adult and I'm responsible for them.

Show your little girl that, unlike your mom, you are able to show up . . . How is she doing with all this information? Good. Relaxing, and feeling less lonely.

So fly this kid up to the present time, with you, through grade school, middle school, high school, college years, meeting Mary, buying the house, all the way up to right now. (I said this all very slowly, with time for her to imagine each phase of life.) *Show her around. Good. Now show her Mary over there. I bet she looks exactly like your Mom.* No, not at all! (Mona laughs.)

Yeah. I know. Can you explain to her about personalities, that Mary is an introvert who needs lots of time alone? (She nods.) *And that doesn't mean she's necessarily mad, or that you're bad?* (She nods.) *Try this: Put your mom's slamming out in one hand, and Mary's cooling out in the other. Hang out with that for a moment. What do you notice?*
They're totally different people with different reasons.

Does the little one understand that, too?
Yeah.

Another stupid therapy question: Which age of you is better equipped to have an adult relationship, the thirty-five-year-old school teacher or the traumatized kid?
(Mona smiles.) That's a hard one. I think the adult.

What do you need to tell that child?
That I'm the one who knows about Mary, and that she needs to ask me what's really happening when she's scared that Mary has left.

How about that she needs to turn to you every single time she gets scared?

That's easier.

*Imagine feeling scared or feeling angry, turning your attention to
that child, checking out the internal and external situation, and
acting from your adult to comfort that child and let her know
what's really going on.*
I can do that.

Is it time to hug that child inside of you?
(Mona hugs herself.) Yeah.

How does that feel?
Good.

Will you be able to feel when that kid part gets activated? (She
nods.) *And will you take care of that kid and point out that this
little blond woman is not your mom and not going anywhere and
that you can talk to her, if you want to?*
Yeah. I can do that.

*Imagine that Mary gets quiet and retreats to the den. Your little
one might start feeling abandoned. What happens?*
I've got her taken care of, but I'm still feeling mad.

*What part is angry? Is it, by any chance, related to your ever-
pissed-off mother?*
Oh God! It's her!

Where do you feel her inside? (Mona runs her hands from her
throat to her belly.)

What color is in there? What substance is that mom anger made out of?
It's like red volcanic lava.

Do you need your mom's anger inside of you?
No.

Are you ready to move it out?
Yes.

Put on some asbestos, fire-proof gloves. When you're ready, scoop that lava out and dump it right there, in the hole in the floor at your feet . . . Keep going until it's all out . . . What percentage did you get?
Sixty-five.

Keep going until it's gone.
(Mona takes about five minutes.) It's all gone!

How do you feel?
Different. Lighter! Like I can breathe!

What would you like there instead?
Peace.

Would you like some safety and acceptance, too?
Oh, yeah.

What color are these things? And what substance are they?
Peace is white. Safety is pink. Acceptance is light green, like

new leaves. And they're all this frothy, whipped cream consistency, all mixed up and very soothing.

*So fill up your whole core with frothy peace, frothy safety, and
frothy acceptance . . . Is the core full?* (She nods.) *Now bring it
through your whole body, every bone, every organ, all the muscle,
all the fat, all the blood: peace, safety, and acceptance. Breathe it
through every cell . . . How is that?*
Amazing. I feel more grown up. Settled and like I can breathe.

*Think about Mary taking alone time with a book in the den. What
do you get now?*
It's not about me. And I think my mom was protecting her
own scared kid that felt like she was bad, just like I've been
doing. I see my mom better, now.

Mary had had tears in her eyes during some of Mona's work and
was smiling at the end of it. I turned to her and asked what it
had been like for her. She replied that she was deeply moved and
much more understanding of what "buttons" she was pushing
when she needed time alone. She agreed that she should continue
to take time, when she needed it, and that she might ask, "How
is your little girl with that?," if Mona looked distressed. She said
that it was scary for her to ask for time alone and that she often
waited until she was completely overloaded before she did.

Mary, how old is the part that's scared?
Lots of ages. Some really little; some are grade school age.

What are they afraid of?

Lots of things. No one yelled at my house. Yelling is really scary. It feels like I'm bad and horrible things are going to happen. (With more questioning she told me the kid parts were worried about violence, abandonment, and being bad.)

What does your adult know about Mona?
I know that she doesn't want to leave me, that she's never violent. And from today's session, I know that her upset is more about her mom than it is about me.

Are you ready to tell the kid parts what you know? (She nods.) *It's story time. Gather all those little parts of you on the couch. Get your arms around all of them. Got them? Good. Can you tell them, in kid language, what you just told me? . . . Add to that, that they've got you, all the time. Whatever mood Mona is in, whatever Mona does, these kiddos live inside of you, are part of you, and always have you, a competent, loving adult to be with them and watch out for them . . . How are they doing?*
Calmer. They get it about not being bad and feel much safer.

Great! Let's imagine some scenarios. First one: You've just come home from a hectic day at work. You're overloaded and depleted and looking forward to some peace and quiet. Your extroverted partner wants to tell you all about her day, and you don't have any space to take in any more. What do you notice?
A little anxiety and a sense of overwhelm.

What do you need to do?
Tell the kids that I'll take care of this. Tell them that they're

okay; I'm okay, no matter what. And then tell Mona what I need.

Can you tell the kids, and then bring the adult forward to practice this conversation with Mona?
(A few minutes later, Mary looks up and then over at Mona.) Honey, I love you, but I just had a hard day at work and I don't have any wavelength left for listening. Can we talk after I've had some rest and some food? I really want to talk to you, but not this minute.

(Mona nods and then sighs.) Yeah, I understand. I know how you are. I'm okay.

(Mary smiles.) Thank you! (Then she sighs in relief.)

How was that?
(Mary:) Okay, I was a little tense, but I kept the kids behind me and was able to reassure Mona, instead of getting too exhausted and waiting until I got mad to say what I wanted. It was good.

(Mona:) Because Mary was so nice, when she said it, my kid didn't feel as abandoned, and I let her know that I was there. It worked okay.

Can both of you acknowledge what you've learned, acknowledge the other one? (Both smile and nod at each other and then high five.) *Now imagine the ten thousand times you're going to reenact this situation, because your very different wiring is unlikely to change.* (Mary smiles. Mona laughs out loud. Both nod.)

MORE TARGETS

||| Differentiating between the habits and expectations from
a former relationship and a current one: *In one hand can you
hold the person you were with your old, violent boyfriend, and
in the other your current self with John, your nice, reasonable
guy? Can you pull that younger self up here and show her who
John really is? What can your current self tell your younger
self about John? . . . Which part of you will know best how
to respond? . . . So which part of you is in charge? . . . Is that
younger part of you ready to be hugged inside and let you deal
with the real John, who isn't perfect, but isn't a jerk?*

||| Differentiating between an idealized mate and the one you
have: *Can you hold that ideal husband in one hand, the one
who loads the dishwasher the correct way, is never anxious,
and always pays close attention to what you need? And hold the
guy you have in the other hand. Hang out with both of these
guys for a moment. What are you feeling now? What does it say
about you that you're with this flawed one? . . . Now that you've
felt the sadness, look over at your guy and what do you see? . . .
That's the one you have. Can you tolerate him? . . . You say you
can love him! Feel it right now.*

||| Pulling out a projection: *Michael, look over at Janice. Can
you see how you've projected your crazy, scary mother onto her?
What color is that projection? Where did you stick it onto her?
It's not hers. Can you reach toward her and pull your projected
mom off of her? Good. Now send that back to your real mom,
where it belongs. Good. Now look at Janice. How does she seem
now?*

RELATIONSHIP SUMMARY

The more I learn about attachment, the more I see baby, child, and parental parts in the best and worst of everyone's relationships, including my own. Helping clients conduct their love lives under the stewardship of their healthiest, most adult parts allows room for true intimacy, good problem solving, conflict resolution, partnership, good sex, and the fun that a good relationship can hold.

CHAPTER 7

Working With Personality Disorders

In the theory of structural dissociation (van der Hart et al., 2006), personality disorders are considered secondary dissociation in which there is one ANP and more than one EP. While somewhat separate, these parts share the same information, with no amnesia or time loss, and have more access to each other than do the parts of DID people. All people with personality disorders suffered inadequate or disrupted early attachment experiences. Many suffered early trauma and abuse. Because of these histories, psychotherapy for people with personality disorders must be done in the context of a safe, attached therapeutic relationship, incorporating therapist availability, firm boundaries, and endless empathy.

BORDERLINE PERSONALITY DISORDER

When thinking about people with borderline personality disorder, imagine an abandoned baby. That baby will start out in a normal, alert, and responsive state (could be the forerunner of the ANP), become agitatedly whiny and clingy (growing into an EP that some call manipulative), become angry (another EP), and then give up, sinking into depression (another EP). If that baby was abused, you could imagine overcompliant or combative states that, with repetition, become strongly ingrained EPs. Your job as a therapist will be to help your client bring the ANP forward to take charge of all parts, and to give each the security of having an ever-present nurturing adult. Because people with borderline personality disorder are sensitive to abandonment, you must emphasize that as they develop a better relationship "inside," with themselves, they get to keep the "outside" relationship with you.

CASE EXAMPLE Borderline Personality Disorder

Margo was raised by drug-addicted parents. Her mother was passive and spaced out. Her father, when he was around, was often abusive. Luckily she'd gotten some adoration and good food when she'd visited her grandmother, who took her on full-time when Margo was ten years old. By that time, Margo's states were fully extant. When I saw her, she was twenty-two and struggling. Margo's ANP was bright, engaging, hardworking, practical, and funny. Her other states (EPs) included a way-too-clingy chooser of bad men, an explosively angry screamer, a suicidally agitated part, and a depressed, passive, nihilistic part.

We started our work with a thorough history, my best calm-down exercises, and discussing the course of therapy. This example is an amalgam of work across several sessions, but you'll get the gist.

Margo, you know that piece of you when you're happy and inter-ested and focused? Would you like to be in that space more of the time?
Well, yeah!

That's going to be job number one for us. After that, we're going to go after all that bad stuff that happened to you and get it out of your system. And after that, we are going to get you operating on all cylinders to do whatever you want in the world (the three steps to healing in phase-oriented treatment [van der Hart et al., 2006]). *How does that sound?*
That works for me.

Great! I want you to think about when you're on your game at work, feeling good, feeling grown-up, and just on it.
Got it. I'm there!

Feel it in your body. Notice the thoughts that go with it, and think of a time when you did a good job taking care of someone who needed it.
My roommate was upset when she broke up with her boy-friend, and I held her when she cried and took care of her.

That's a great example. I want you to hold onto this state of mind while we think of another part of you. Remember when you wanted to see me on the weekend, and I said no? What were you feeling right then?
Really scared, and then really mad.

How old did that feel?

Pretty little . . . maybe three or four.

Can you see and feel that little Margo, who got left alone so many times?
I can! She's a mess!

What does she need?
She needs someone to show up!

Can this mature, caring, twenty-two-year-old show up for her?
(She sighs.) I guess.

Try this. Walk up to that little one, introduce yourself, and pick her up. Do you have her? Great. Tell her some things. Tell her that she will always have an adult around, from now on. That's you. Tell her she'll never be alone, that every time she's freaking out, she needs to look around for you, her grown-up. You feel that little body on your lap. Let her feel your strong arms around her. Look her in the eyes. What's going on?
She's calming down.

That's great! Let's calm her down even more. I want her to feel who else was around for her. Can you fly her up to ten, when you moved to your grandma's? Show her all the ways and all the years that your grandma showed up for you. Show this little one how your grandma is still there for you (modified life span integration [Pace, 2007]). *And show that little one how all your grandma's good love and caring got into the grown-up you. Show her how you know how to hug and talk to people who are upset.*
Wow! I guess I do have that. That's cool!

So bring that little one all the way to right here and right now. How's she doing now?

Good! She feels good, and I feel good.

Are you ready to pledge to be there for her forever?

Yes, I'm ready.

Take her hands, look her in the eyes. Do you, Margo, promise to take care of your little scared part and to provide her grown-up caring and attention when she needs it?

(She giggles.) I do.

Margo, ask your inside kid if she pledges to look for the adult in you first, when she needs to feel loved and connected.

She does.

Good job! Let's think of some times when this kid part might arise and you're going to take extra care with her. What do you think?

When you (her therapist) go on vacation, when Grandma's not around, when my roommate is gone, if someone doesn't show up—stuff like that.

What could you do, before this kid part of you freaks out?

I can remind her and remind myself that I'm not four and that I'm okay.

Good idea. Let's practice, right now. Imagine that I'm out of town the same week that your grandma and your roommate are gone. It's Friday night, and you don't know what you're doing for the weekend. You can feel the desperation coming on . . . What do you do now?

I remind myself that I'm a grown-up and make some plans.

Those are good ideas. What happens if the big loneliness comes in anyway and you start feeling desperate?
I look inside for that little girl part. When I find her, I pick her up and have her really notice that I'm still here and she's not alone, and that it's not fun, but I can hack it. I make sure she feels me hugging her. And I don't go looking for any old guy to hug me, like I usually do.

You get an A on this lesson! Sometimes people tell me that they don't want to take care of their inside little parts, because they're tired of having to do it all. What do you think?
I think those people are still feeling from their little kid space, and they're still mad that people weren't there. I get mad, too. You know I do. But I know if I don't learn to do it, I'm going to keep being upset all the time, and enough of me is grown up to do it this way.

Over the course of two years we continued this work, mixed with EMDR, emotional support, and skill building. The hardest part to contain, for both Margo and me, was her "angry screamer." We did the containment work, when she was calm, and planned for work, by future pacing both the appearance and the containment of this angry part: *Margo, right now, your nurturing, strong adult is doing a great job of holding onto that rage-filled kid part. Some day I'm going to mess up, or otherwise trigger your anger. When that happens, I want to help you find your strongest, best adult to take over and handle that kid part and that situation.*

Two weeks later I hurt my back and had to do my sessions reclined on the office couch, where Margo had always sat. Most other clients took the situation in stride. Margo exploded at the perceived loss of my presence:

I'm not here to take care of you! Who do you think I am?!

I think you're a very distressed Margo, who might be triggered into thinking I'm like her drugged out parents. I'm very sorry that my prone position is triggering you so much, and I'm very glad that we get to work with your angry part today.
Fuck you!

Sorry, I never do that with my clients, but I do hold them to prior agreements . . . Remember when we made a deal to bring your adult forward to contain the angry part. This is the day to do that. Are you ready?
I guess.

I want the oldest, wisest, strongest, and most nurturing Margo to come forth. Bring up that part of you that you mostly are at work, and bring up the best version. Bring forth that great driver, great friend, and great wrangler of inside parts.
(With a big sigh, Margo starts shifting before my eyes.) Okay, I'm here.

Good job! Take a few more breaths . . . and now tell me about this angry part. What's going on?
She thinks you're not here. She thinks you're like them, my

parents, and things are going to get bad, and you're going to hurt me or go away.

No wonder she's distressed! It sounds like she's forgotten that she's got the grown-up that counts. How old is she?
She's lots of ages. There are some really little babies, all the way to teenager.

Can you turn that child around until she's looking at you, and explain who you are to her?
Hi, inside kids. You may not remember me, but I'm grown-up, twenty-four-year-old Margo. You've got me now, always around, never drunk, never on drugs. (She turns to look at me.) You know what, Robin? Some of these kid parts weren't here when we did this before.

Margo, give them a tour of your adult life so they know who you are: your apartment, your roommate, your job, your car, and how you function now.
. . . Done!

What do you need to tell these angry parts?
They need to know that we're safe and that I'm not going anywhere.

Tell them. Then tell them how you deal with anger now.
(She is silent, and then she breaths deeply. Her shoulders drop, and her eyes open.) I let them know they were safe and that they lived in me and my life is okay. Then I did some

breathing and relaxing. Then I told them that you were here, even if you're lying down. I showed them that you came to work, even though you're hurting. Then they sort of melted together, and then sort of went away.

Wow! Look what happens when we can deal with these states with some adult awareness! That's very cool! Tell me more!
If we didn't do that when I was mad, we wouldn't have all the pieces.

I think you're right. And I think there are more angry pieces that might come out with a different kind of threat. Do you agree?
That makes sense. I'll have to think about it.

In the meantime, what can you do when you get mad?
If I'm not in my adult, I'm not going to remember to breathe and ground. I need to feel mad and then find my grown-up, and then feel angry but not blow up.

Next time, let's do a search through your whole being for the other angry parts and find out ages and what brings up the anger. Let's get all the angry young parts connected up with your adult.

And so we did. For the last six months of therapy, we worked on Margo bringing her adult perspective and here-and-now self to new situations. During this time, she found new capacities for being alone, dealing with setbacks, and letting her "oldest, wisest" twenty-five-year-old self choose a safe, sane, and financially sound man.

WORKING WITH NARCISSISTIC CLIENTS

Imagine a baby in a busy household. Imagine the baby gets lonely, cries for attention, and gets no response. After crying itself to sleep, the baby awakens to its parents' connection and praise. The baby gets fed by the clock, not its feeling of hunger. It is praised for accomplishments and for showing a happy face. When it is not performing or not happy, it is ignored. Little by little, the child learns that there is no response to its true needs, that attachment is predicated on performance, and that being "good" is all that matters. If this baby is beaten or abused when it shows any defiance or even negative emotion, the lesson becomes even stronger: "I am lovable only when I am perfect" (Kernberg, 1993; Kohut, 1971; Manfield, 1992).

According to James Masterson (1981), if the child rejects the needy, empty, "unlovable" part and decides that it is in fact the perfect, always lovable, always right, deserving-of-attention part, it becomes an "exhibitionist" narcissist. This is the self-aggrandizing, scheming, and quick-to-take-offense character in every sit-com. This person cannot take negative feedback, needs all available attention, needs to be in control, and maintains a mask of competency and puffed-up worth that hides a huge sense of shame, futility, emptiness, and fear. In contrast, Masterson's "closet" narcissists are in touch with the shame and emptiness, may think everyone else has the same feelings, and attempt to get recognition by pleasing everyone around them in order to be seen and treated as good enough.

Through the lenses of the theory of structural dissociation (van der Hart et al., 2006) and polyvagal theory (Porges, 2011), we see ANPs carrying the work of functioning in the world and the heavy load of staying puffed up (exhibitionist) or keeping anxiously, codependently hunkered down (closet) in a defensively mobilized state. Both kinds of ANPs are defending against anyone seeing the collapsed, shame-filled, empty, and hopeless EP in its immobilized/dorsal vagal state.

Psychotherapy with narcissistic clients can be difficult because they are terrified that they will be seen as the miserable scum that deep inside they believe they are. Classical exhibitionist narcissists are generally well defended from knowing their hopeless, needy, empty parts. They may have achieved big things in their lives and crave the attention that goes with that achievement. Clients may take offense and become offensive if you try to show their other sides too early in the work. Closet narcissists may be too busy charming you into liking them to reach down deep to do the work. (And, of course, these defenses are not mutually exclusive.)

Because deep work can be threatening to these clients, you must make sure that the therapeutic relationship can stand the work. Make sure your clients know that you are absolutely in their corners. They must know you like them. And they must know that you can stand them, even when they are angry, hopeless, and not looking "good" or impressive.

CASE EXAMPLE An Exhibitionist Narcissist

Jack was fifty and intelligent and was an accomplished, wealthy entrepreneur and a "drug-along spouse" whose wife gave him an ultimatum: "Come with me to therapy or give me a divorce." His narcissism was clear to me in the first minutes of the couple's session. He was too charming (a defense), unable to truly see or hear his wife (a deficit), arrogant (a defense), condescending (a defense), and overconcerned with being "right" and making his wife "wrong" (a huge defense). In the second session, we did genograms (Kitchur 2005, 2010) on both clients: family trees with personal histories of trauma and support. As I suspected, he came from a striving immigrant family with no room for imperfection, play, or connection. His mother was anxious and overdirective. His father was abusive, in the name of discipline. Both parents worked, and he was often alone.

Here is what I said to him, first acknowledging the ANP: *Jack, do you know how amazing you are? Your childhood was an emotional desert, and look how you've come through it all! Look at your business, your amazing wife, and how put together you are.* Then, acknowledging, lightly, the EP: *I think your parents, in their focus on survival, didn't grow some skills in your brain that you probably need. They didn't teach you how to deal with feelings, yours or hers* (nodding toward his wife). *Would you want to gain some of those skills? I would love the opportunity to work with you and boot up some new software into that big brain of yours.* (How could he resist?)

The therapy was complex, partly because it is easy to scare narcissistic clients out of therapy. They are often torn between loving the attention and hating to be seen. They can be hard on therapists, too: demanding, attacking, and soooo entitled. We got more history, and I had Jack hang out many times with his emotions tied to those past events, starting with feeling for less than a minute. I told him that we were strengthening the hardware in his brain to be able to hold emotion, so that we could do the deep work. I used myself as circuit builder, asking, *What's it like to feel that shame and to know that it breaks my heart that your father said that to you?* (Fosha, 2000). Sometimes, I had him hold my gaze and notice me being present with him, while feeling the old emotions (Sheldon & Sheldon, 2010). We did EMDR with some of the egregious injuries, once he had some tolerance for his feelings. This all worked. He felt better, and less triggered, but most of his defenses still separated his suave adult from his hurting kid.

Six months into therapy, we started doing ego state therapy. We had a good therapeutic relationship. As Jack's presenting ANP began to trust me to like him and support him, we spent more time "inside" the distressed parts. First I explained the work:

Jack, you have some loose circuits inside that need to get wired together. I want to use technical language from psychology, because I think that you, with your big brain, will understand it. I might default to simpler language later. Let me know if that bothers you. (I'm still telling him that he's special enough to get the real story.) *The theory of structural dissociation says that kids like you were split into two parts, the apparently normal part, or ANP, and the emotional part, or EP. The ANP, in your case, was the perfect kid. He was smart, took care of himself, and excelled at everything. The EP, or maybe more than one EP, held all the needs that your parents didn't notice or meet. In the EP, as in every kid and every human* (normalizing), *are the feelings of loneliness, shame, emptiness, and all the needs for attention. The job of the ANP, aside from functioning, is to feel good. And in order to feel good, the ANP's job is to avoid anything about the EP like the plague.*

(Jack nods along the whole time.) *Jack, I think you're get-*

ting this. I saw you hold your breath when I talked about those EP feelings. What do you notice inside, right now?

I'm feeling a little tight, like anxiety, and a lot like changing the subject.

Changing the subject would be a great ANP move. How good would it feel, zero to ten, to change the subject, avoid thinking about all those old feelings, and stay with feeling good?

It would feel really good, a nine or ten.

Stay with that, and watch this. (I did several EMDR sweeps to clear some of Jack's inappropriate positive affect [Knipe, 2005] from the ANP. After about six rounds of eye movements, the positive feelings had plummeted. There are other ways to get to this point, but this is the fastest one I know.)

So, Jack, when you think about avoiding those EP feelings, what do you notice now?

I don't want to. I don't want to be run by avoidance anymore. I want to feel the damn stuff and get over it.

So you're ready to feel and ready to connect these neural circuits?

I'm ready! (using his strong, low, decisive, executive voice).

Yes, sir! Me too! Here's what we do. Feel the part of you that voice came from: strong, grown up, and in charge. Where do you feel that strength in your body?

(Jack thumps his chest and his arms, sitting up very straight.)

Hold onto that. We're going to need it. I want to take a trip with you back fifty-one years. A boy child was born in a hospital. He's

*in a little crib with your name on it. Go in and pick that child up
and bring him here . . . Got him?*
Yup.

*Look into the eyes of that little one. Feel his weight in your hands.
Hear his breathing and noises. And while you're doing that, that
kid is seeing you, feeling your strong, grown-up hands holding
him, hearing your voice, and knowing that he has your attention.
What's it like, holding that infant you?* (Much of this comes
from imaginal nurturing work [Steele, 2007a].)
It's familiar, because I've held my children, but different,
more loaded, because this one is me.

*I want you to mine your experiences with your kids for your care
of this one . . . It's time to admire him. See his perfect toes and
fingers; his adorable baby face, his sweet round baby body, and
the intelligence behind those brown eyes. Notice him noticing
you adoring him. Let that feeling go back and forth between
you. That's called intersubjectivity, two people connected and
feeling the same thing. Hang out with that. Now I want you
to notice how little and fragile he is and that he is full of needs.
He needs milk, warmth, diaper changes, company, cuddles, and
constant attention. Unfrown your face and say to that baby,
"No matter what you need, you're perfect. You're lovable even
if you wake me up at three A.M. You're lovable even if you pee
in my face. You're a perfectly fine baby, worthy of my love and
attention, no matter what you feel and what you need." And I
want you to embody that love for everything about this child.
Are you feeling it?*
This is a little harder, but I'm doing it.

Unconditional love isn't easy, but this kid didn't get it in round one and definitely needs it now. See the whole child: intelligence, needs, crying, adorableness. If you can hold all that, you can tolerate all of yourself. Feel him, look at him, and let him know you're there.
I got it. I'm doing it. He's settling down because he knows I'm there. I used to hand the kids off to my wife when they got needy. It's because I couldn't be that way. Shit!

Let's deal directly with your regret and how you're going to be with your kids later. Right now, let's make up for it with this baby. See the whole baby, the smart parts, the cute parts, and the messy, needy parts. It's all or nothing.
I can love him. He's all right.

That's great. Hang out with that for a while . . . Now, it's time to grow this kid up. I want you to take this kid through every year of your life, pouring on the love and attention that he needed in each year (a variation on life span integration [Pace, 2007]). This will be at lightning speed. Ready? Take him through that first year. See yourself picking up the lonely baby, feeding him when he's hungry, and connecting with him when he's unhappy . . . Now the second year. He wants endless games of peek-a-boo, lots of play, really poopy diapers changed, and a good rocking when he's sad . . . Now the third year, he's learning "No!" He can really yell. Admire that, and see the neediness under that.

We took him all that way through childhood, and hit some specific distressing incidents, and Jack was up to the task of connecting. When we got to his twenties, we lumped years together.

As we went through the years, he found more things that he regretted. Finally we got to the present.

> *Jack, I want you to see the man you are now. You're powerful, you look pretty good for fifty-one, and you're still smart. You also are allowing yourself to see your insecurities, your fears, and the ways you've messed up. Can you see this man, you? Can you see all of him, put your strong hands on his shoulders, look him in the eye, and give him your acceptance and loving attention? Can you tell him that he's good enough, even though you see his flaws? Can you tell him that he's lovable anyway?*

Yes, I can do that. (His voice, not for the first time in this exercise, is breaking.) Robin, this is unprecedented in my life. It feels bizarre, but right. It feels important.

> *Jack, we still have work to do, but this day will be the springboard for all the rest. Before I throw you out for the day, there's one more thing to do. Can you look at that grown-up Jack who holds all your ages from infant to now? Good. Are you ready to open your arms wide and hug all those ages of you inside? Great! What does that feel like?*

(With a big sigh, Jack smiles.) I feel like me, but in a different way. I think I'm more relaxed, and not on guard.

The therapy continued for six more months. We spent more time with different pivotal ages. Jack was able to tolerate his regrets for what he didn't have and for the distress he caused others. He was able to forgive himself his imperfections, noting that he and the other people all survived and that he had been unaware of his reflexive need to seem perfect and be appreciated.

Jack changed. He became more relaxed in many aspects of his life: much less worried about how he was seen, more responsive to other people's needs and his own, and more playful and responsive with his wife, his nearly grown kids, and his employees. His wife was pleased. We invited her in for a session, near the end, and she told him about the many changes she had seen: "You're so much less defensive! You notice other people's feelings. And you feel 'real' to me, like the mask is down. You're more patient with everyone. I like you better this way!"

OTHER DISORDERS

Histrionic people have low self-esteem and strive desperately to get attention from the people around them. They are often impulsive and often put a lot of attention into their appearance. They can be exhausting but entertaining clients. Work to develop an adult part that can let all the ages know that they

III   are lovable without having to do anything,
III   are able to get attention from their own internal adult, and
III   can let their adult part connect with other people as a grown-up.

Avoidant and schizoid people tend to spend a lot of time alone. Avoidant people are nearly always full of self-loathing due to early attachment deficits or abuse. While they crave connection, for them, "other people are scary and won't like me anyway, so why bother." Schizoid people tend to be very inward, prone to introspection, and not that interested in others. There can be overlap between these two diagnoses, and they often avoid therapy. When working with these clients, I find their most adult parts and spend a lot of time connecting younger parts with adult parts. Sometimes it is necessary to teach the adult parts, step by step, how to connect with and take care of different ages. When the kid parts are contained, settled, and connected, we explore the adult needs for connection, often using their connection with me as a reference: *What's it like when you know that you have my full attention? Where do you feel that inside?* After a lot of therapy, when it is no longer scary and it feels good: *Do you want to have this experience out in the world?* After working through the fear of that, we make sure to sweep the kid parts back and let the adult part lead the way, and they begin to make more relationships outside of therapy. Some of these clients were so relationship-phobic that I suggest they get dogs. After being consistently loved and happily greeted by their dogs, they develop a more social adult part that can risk connecting with other humans.

Expect long therapies with people who have these diagnoses. It is not unusual to work from two to six years, or even longer, to rewire their brains for good attachment, affect regulation, self-esteem, and social skills. I usually use most of my therapeutic toolbox with these clients, including EMDR, somatic and attachment therapies, and of course ego state therapy.

It is easier to work with these notoriously difficult clients when you can see their deficits as distressed baby parts. Dealing with the shame-filled child beneath the dismissive narcissistic ANP or the angry kid with the personable ANP of a borderline client gives us very human therapists a way to connect and attach to these sometimes hard-to-love clients.

CHAPTER 8

Working With Suicidal Clients

Ego state work can be essential in treating suicidal ideation and the feelings of worthlessness and despair that often accompany it. Self-destructive thoughts often arise from younger parts, and clients are often "split" between an old compulsion to die and a current will to live.

Statistics about suicide in the United States

- Thirty percent of people in the United States have contemplated suicide (NIMH, 2009).
- Around thirty thousand Americans successfully commit suicide each year. Many of these people never went to therapy (NIMH, 2009).
- Risk factors include prior attempts, a family or personal history of mental or substance disorder or violence, exposure to another person's suicide, sexual trauma, loss, and incarceration. Other factors include PTSD, poor attach-

ment, poor social connectedness, and "difference" from cultural expectations (income, disability, ethnicity, sexual or gender difference, victim of bullying).

||| Suicidal ideation may occur in any diagnosis but is most prevalent in people with depression and people on the dissociative spectrum, from PTSD to personality disorders to DID. Bipolar disorder and psychotic disorders often generate suicidal thoughts, feelings and behavior, too.

||| Women attempt suicide three times more than men. Four times more men die by suicide, mostly because they use guns. Fifty percent of all suicides involve a firearm in the home (NIMH, 2009).

ASSESSMENT

When assessing clients for suicide, listen carefully to both your clients and your own gut. Clients may deny thoughts or plans of killing themselves due to shame or due to wanting to keep the suicide option open. Dissociative clients may have parts that don't know about the suicidal ideation and plans of other parts. If you know your client well and know yourself well, and the hair on the back of your neck keeps rising, persist in your questions.

Ask about suicidal thoughts or behavior with most clients during your initial assessment. *Have you ever thought about killing yourself?* If yes, *Have you ever attempted suicide? . . . Tell me about that.* Or *What kept you alive? What part or parts of you wanted to die? . . . How old was that part? Was it trying to kill you, or just trying to stop the bad feelings? What part or parts of you wanted to live? How did they keep you alive?* Because you may be calling on this information later, note it carefully.

Questions for currently suicidal clients

III *Is it thoughts that you should be dead, like you're worthless, or a feeling that you can't stand, or something else?*

III *What part or parts of you are telling you this? Tell me about them.*

III *How old are these?* (Often they are quite young.)

III *How did they get the message that they shouldn't exist?* (Often this comes from abuse and neglect by parents or from a programmed message from organized abuse.) *What was happening then?*

III *Are there other parts of you that want to be alive? Tell me about them.*

III *What does your most grown-up adult think about it.*

III *What can that adult tell those other parts? . . . Can you show these parts who is in your life now? What kind of support you have now? . . . Can you bring those kids up here and show the kinds of messages you get now from people?*

III *Who do you want in charge, the young* (state age) *suicidal part of you, or your* (current age) *adult? . . . How can your adult keep those kids cared for, contained, and safe, and stay alive until we meet again?* (Help client make a plan.)

CASE EXAMPLE "Not Good Enough to Live"

Janelle's parents were anxious, critical, and extremely controlling. She was overapologetic, obsequious, codependent, and unable to stand up for herself. Her parents had let her know that she wasn't a planned child and that her birth was a financial hardship for them. Janelle had been bullied and sexually assaulted by schoolmates and isolated at work. She lived in a sea of shame and social anxiety. In therapy, we had been working on the trauma of her parents' behavior and the bullying. Janelle was fairly dissociated but not DID; an old diagnosis, dependent personality disorder, a variant of borderline, fit her perfectly. When Janelle's job was threatened, she became suicidal. She did not have a specific plan but noticed that she thought about swerving her car into traffic or about slicing her wrists when she was driving or in the kitchen.

Janelle, what thoughts go with the suicidal ones?
I'm a failure. My boss doesn't want me. Nobody does. It's hopeless.

Could you go inside for a moment and notice what percent of you is thinking that?
About 60 percent.

And can you tell me what age those you're-worthless-and-you-should-be-dead thoughts are coming from?
From about five to twenty-five.

Let's start with your five-year-old self. We know how she received that message.
You know that it's from my parents; they didn't want me. Nothing I did was good enough.

And your thirty-five-year-old self, what's her perspective?
My parents were crazy. My dad was so anxious that he had to control everything.

And what's your adult perspective on that five-year-old?
She's a really good kid. It wasn't her fault that her parents were that way. She deserved to be loved better.

Absolutely! Should we go get her and let her know? (She nods.) *And should we get all the other ages of you on the way?* (She nods again.) *Before we go back, can you tell me some reasons your adult wants to be alive, in the here and now?*
My daughter, I could never leave her alone. My husband is a big reason. And knowing that every time I feel terrible, I end up feeling better, after a while.

What else keeps you alive?
(Janelle's eyes fill with tears.) I know God loves me and wants me to live. When I was little, I thought that God was only scary and wanted to punish me. Now I know that he loves me.

Where do you feel that sense of God's love inside? (Janelle puts her hands on her heart and her solar plexus.) *Breathe that in and now breathe that in to every cell in your body. Notice any place that needs an extra dose* (Elizabeth Turner, personal communication, 2006).

Now let's bring this to the little ones. Can your adult fly down the years to that five-year-old? Have your adult pick up that distressed little girl and get her out of that house. Reach out your arms to her and pull her up the years, bringing all the ages of her who got the message that they shouldn't be alive all the way up to right here and right now . . . Now let her know what you know about

*her goodness . . . Bring that strong sense of God's love to this child
. . . Introduce her to that circle of people who love you. Who is in
that circle?*
My circle has my husband, my daughter, you, my friend Betty,
and both dogs.

Do all those beings see you as a good person?
Yes.

Do they think you deserve to live?
Yes.

Can you show that to the younger one? . . . How is she feeling now?
She's relieved and relaxed.

What does she know now that she didn't know before?
She knows that it wasn't her fault everyone was unhappy and
mean. And she knows that it's okay to be alive.

*Great! Can you give that little girl a tour of right here and right
now? Show her this office, your car, your house, you parenting
your kid and laughing with your husband, and you at your job
. . . Show her how functional you are in all those places . . . And
let her know that you're good at being in charge, and that you're
the grown-up who is in charge of her. (And that you're much
nicer and more attentive than your/her parents.) . . . Can she
stay here with you? Will you take care of her? . . . How is she
doing now?*
She gets that she lives here with me and that life is going to be
way easier. She knows that I'm okay and she's okay.

Notice your posture right now!

Wow! I'm sitting up taller than I ever do. I feel stronger and more grown up!

I noticed! . . . Is it time to bring that much more healed child inside of you?

I'm ready!

Hug her inside with both arms . . . How does she feel inside of you?

Safe and warm and loved.

How often are you going to check in with her to make sure she's still safe, still knows it's okay to live, and still knows that things are different now?

I'll connect with her when I wake up, before I sleep, and anytime I feel like I'm bad.

When is she most likely to show up in your everyday life?

She might pop up whenever I get rejected, or if I make a mistake.

What should you do then?

I should remind her that I'm okay, and people can make mistakes without being bad. I remember that two-hand thing you had me do with "I made a mistake" in one hand and "I <u>am</u> a mistake" in the other one. I'll remind her and me that those aren't the same things. And if someone rejects me, then it doesn't mean I'm bad. That's their opinion.

Sounds great! Are there any ages of you feeling like dying or hurting themselves, now?

No, they're all settled down.

Even the twenty-five-year-old?
I swept her up to now with the rest of them. She settled down when she was reminded of my nice husband.

Good job!
Thank you.

CASE EXAMPLE An Intolerable Experience

Charlie was in his mid-forties, slight, sensitive, and intelligent and had a childhood history of neglect by his bipolar mother, bullying by his peers, and too much time by himself. As an adult, he had a small business and a small circle of friends and had just broken up with his girlfriend. When he was cheated by a brutish, threatening contractor, he came unglued. A friend insisted he come to therapy when she noticed his suicidal ideation and withdrawal. He was experiencing unbearable anxiety. The suicidal thoughts were tied with a sense of being trapped and hopeless, with no relief. After a brief intake, which showed that he had suicidal thoughts, with a vague plan, and was in no imminent danger, this is what happened:

Charlie, what's it like inside of you when you think of that horrible interaction with that contractor?
I feel small, and like I'm about to get killed.

Terrified and little?
Yeah.

Did you ever feel like that before?

I felt that my whole childhood, especially at junior high or away from home. Guys would just punch me. Sometimes a group of guys would punch me or taunt me.

I'm so sorry! My heart breaks for that kid you were . . . What's it like knowing that I have empathy for that kid you were and the adult you are? (ego state modification of Fosha, 2000).
It's weird but feels good. Nobody was ever there to express anything like that.

Do you know that there should have been someone there?
Yes, I do know that. I see the way they raise kids now, and I realize that I was feral. My mom was crazy, and my dad was gone all the time, at work.

I know you haven't been to therapy before. I'd like to do some talking to pieces of you, to bring the here-and-now information you have as an adult to all the rest. Is it okay if we do something weird?
You're the doctor.

And you're an adult that gets to make decisions for himself. (I'm building a sense of agency in his adult, because he seems too compliant.)
Okay. I want to try it. (In a much stronger, more adult voice.)

Okay, me too! . . . I want that adult you are to look back at that terrified kid, who never knew when he'd get humiliated or beat down, and who never had anyone to protect him . . . Do you see

him? (He nods.) *Can you feel him?* (He nods and tears up.) *Can you feel compassion for that kid?*
Yes, it's like I can feel his fear and feel bad that he's having the fear.

Great! I'd like you, in adult mode, to travel back to that place, noticing that none of those bullies would dare try anything with an adult around, and talk to that kid.
Okay.

Are you back there? (He nods.) *Tell that kid that you see what's going on and that you, as an adult, know that he should have been protected. Tell him that, even though you run into assholes, no one has laid a hand on you in—how many years?*
It's been about twenty-five years.

Can you show that kid how many years it's been, and how much safer you are these days?
Done!

Can you make it clear to him that you have much more control of most of your life now?
Got it.

And can you let that kid know that he lives up here in the twenty-first century with you? Show him your condo, your dog, those friends you mentioned, your business, and your car. (Charlie sits up more in his chair and looks more adult and more relaxed.) *What are you feeling right now?*

I feel like I'm "here" for the first time in days. I feel like I can breathe. And I'm going to sue that son of a—never mind—that threatened me.

What happened to the suicidal feelings?
Gone! And I'm mad instead.

Great! Hang out with the mad for a while. It looks good on you! I notice that you've made fists. Can we try something?
I'm ready!

Can you put one of those fists into my hands and very slowly push, feeling all the sensations that go with doing that? Remember, don't kill the therapist!
Gladly.
(While Charlie slowly and strongly pushes into my hands, first one hand and then the other, I coach him to notice the sensations and stay present. Then we bring in more ego state components.) *Charlie, can you find that kid who never got to punch back and let him feel the strength in your adult arms?* (He nods, looking fascinated.) *Could you let that kid know that it's okay to be angry, to feel it, and to feel strong?* (He breathes, shivers for a moment, and straightens up, pushing a bit harder.) *Does the adult know it, too?*
Oh, yeah! (in a strong voice).

What are you getting now?
I'm getting that I didn't know I could defend myself. I didn't even know I could be mad! I had no backup then, and I got that confused with now.

My arms are tired. May we stop the pushing?
Sure.

How's that kid part of you?
He's barely there. He's okay, but he's <u>me</u> now.

That's what we want . . . What did you learn here?
A lot in a short time. I learned that I'm not a kid anymore,
that it's okay to be mad, that it's okay to defend myself, and
that I can. And I learned that I had—what do you call it?—
PTSD from my childhood that was affecting me now. And
I learned that if this stuff comes up again, I'm coming to see
you again.

That works for me!
Me, too!

SUICIDAL IDEATION WITH HIGHLY DISSOCIATIVE CLIENTS

The more dissociative a client is, the more separation there will
be between parts. The "adult" part of a client may not be aware
of suicidal or self-destructive alters or may view them with dis-
trust and avoidance rather than compassion. According to the
theory of structural dissociation (van der Hart et al., 2006),
after building up the ANPs (apparently normal or adult parts),
you need to get them connected with, caring for, and in control
of all other parts (the EPs). With acutely suicidal alters, this
needs to be done quickly and, if needed, with more than one
part.

Interventions

III Get the ANP in on the conversation: *Can I talk to that smart lawyer part of you, the one who just won that case?*

III Check for all the parts wanting to live and all the parts with the compulsion to die. *Go inside and find the parts of you that want to be alive, present, and go on with life. What parts do you find?* (You might get "None" if the distressed alter is running the show, in which case you might make sure you ask for the ANP to do the search.) *Take a poll and ask them what they're staying alive for. I'll make a list, as you tell me . . . Good. Now let's give those distressed parts a chance to talk: When you go inside, which parts of you want to commit suicide? How old are they? Are there parts voting for death in order to stop the pain? Are there parts voting for death because they don't deserve to live? Are there other reasons?* (With survivors of ritual abuse or mind control, there may be parts programmed to kill the body if the client "tells" or breaks other rules of the abusive organization, or on specific dates.)

III Get the ANP that's in charge to take care of the needs of the distressed parts, orient them to now, and set the rules. If the ANP is overwhelmed or abhors the parts, you can use a modified safe place to take care of the suicidal part or parts (see Chapter 3).

III Make sure you have all the suicidal parts taken care of, in agreement to live, or contained.

CASE EXAMPLE A Suicidal DID Client

Bonnie was thirty-five and divorced. After a few months of therapy she was newly diagnosed as a multifragmented DID client.
She was bright, funny, and engaging in a childlike way, except
when she was in radically different states. We discovered that
she was survivor of ritualized group sexual abuse and torture at
the age of four, that her mother had been similarly abused, and
that Bonnie had suffered periodic sexual abuse by her maternal
grandfather. Her older brother, Lennie, whom we imagined
had the same abuse, had recently taken his own life. Some of
her many child parts wanted to "go where Lennie went." Some
wanted to die to stop the pain of the grief. Some wanted to die
to stop the abuse. (DID parts often experience the events of the
past as happening right now. They are, as Kurt Vonnegut writes
in *Slaughterhouse Five*, "unstuck in time.") Her adult parts (in
true DID fashion, she had several) generally wanted to be alive,
though one thought living with all these other parts was a "big
hassle." This example is after ten years of intensive therapy:

(To the ANP:) *Bonnie, can you close your eyes, look inside, and
get all your parts to the Talking Place, for a meeting?*
I don't want to, but I will.

Great! Let me know when you're all there (another fun play on
words with DID).
Okay, what are we talking about?

*You're going to need a strong grown-up coalition to deal with this
suicide threat. Who would be the best parts of you to deal with this?*

I need me, Bonnie; my motherly part that's a lot like you; my fighter part, even though she's younger; and my organizer part.

Who is running this committee?
The organizer.

Can you ask the organizer to bring up the parts that are the most self-destructive, so that we can help keep them safe and meet their needs?
(After a long pause:) The worst one is a little girl who can't stand living without Lennie. She wants to be with him, and she doesn't want to feel sad.

What part is going to take care of her?
Organizer assigns the motherly one that's like you to hold the little girl and let her be sad, but not hurt us.

Good pick and good plan! Who's next?
The naked, bleeding girl is the one who felt all the bad things. She missed Lennie when she was in the Place (the cult foster home). So him being gone is like she's there and the bad things are happening . . . She can't stand it and wants to be dead.

Who is going to take care of her?
I am and the motherly part is. First, we're picking her up out of the Place. Then, we're going to bring her to now and show her around, that there's no abuse here. Then we're going to clean her up in the Healing Pool and dress her, and the

motherly part is going to hold her and make her feel the good hugs. We're going to let her know that even though Lennie isn't here, and we're sad, the abuse isn't still happening.

Make it so. (Star Trek language abounds in this client's therapy.) . . . *Who else needs some help?*
I don't know, but they don't want to be here and don't want you to know about them.

Bonnie, can you and the organizer go inside and find them?
(After a long pause, and some distressed and then stern looks, Bonnie opens her eyes.) These want us to be dead because we told (about the abuse) and because we are evil and make bad things happen. They say it's time to die. These are like ones we dealt with before. And they're really big and really scary.

Remember when we talked about introjects? You've found some more. I want you and the organizer and the fighter in on this. Can you go over to the biggest, meanest one, and find the zipper on her back? . . . Can you unzip that zipper? What do you find underneath?
A little one. A little one that's scared and wants to be safe and carries the message.

Can you all thank this little girl for trying to help all these years by getting you to behave in a safe way, for that time? . . . And can you rescue her and bring her up to now, where it's safe?
The motherly one is holding her and hugging her and telling her that she doesn't have to die, since the bad people aren't here.

How is she doing?
Much better.

Are there more than one of them?
Yes.

You know what to do.
(Bonnie closes her eyes for a while.) No one wants to kill themselves anymore, and the ones that thought they have to kill us, because we're bad, are fading into us. That's a good trick with the zippers.

How are you doing with the sadness now?
I feel terrible, but more grown-up terrible. We weren't seeing each other anyway, and he was crazier than I am, which is saying something. But I miss him, and it's awful not to ever be able to see him.

How is the sad little girl?
Okay and sitting on the lap of the motherly part, feeling sad, but kind of good sad.

How is the part that felt all the abuse?
She's clean and not hurting, and also sitting on the motherly part's lap, and she knows that it's not happening now, but she's not very trusting.

Keep showing her that it's now, until she gets more used to the idea

. . . So back to everyone at the Talking Place. Do we have a consensus about living?
Y̶o̶u̶ ̶e̶x̶c̶e̶p̶t̶ for all the goddamn hassle of dealing with all of this!

What's the plan?
Staying alive to see what happens next!

That works for me!
Me, too.

Twenty-five years later, this client called to tell me that she had almost died from blood clots in her lungs. At the hospital, she'd had time to think about her life and realized that "my life was worth living and I was worthwhile, and I wouldn't have known this if I hadn't worked with you." We were both teary on the phone as we discussed this miracle.

EGO STATE THERAPY IS NOT ALL YOU NEED

- If your clients cannot realistically promise to keep themselves safe, you may need to get them to a hospital.
- If hospitalization isn't possible, you may bring in your client's family or friends to make a care team and a plan to keep safe.
- Know the crisis lines, hospitals, and other resources in your community, for your clients or for you to contact as needed.
- When working with suicidal clients, make sure that you are getting good, supportive consultation.

||| Document everything you do. Suicide is the number one reason for lawsuits against therapists.

SUICIDAL CLIENTS: SUMMARY

Whatever brings clients to your office is "a part that wants to live." Helping suicidal clients differentiate between the hopeless, overwhelmed pieces of themselves and the resourced, forward-thinking pieces is helpful, whatever the circumstances. Containing the often younger and often traumatized parts that want to die and connecting them to internal and external resources can bring the wherewithal to continue to live and continue to heal.

CHAPTER 9

Working With Cultural, Familial, and Abuse-Related Introjects

People absorb identity, thoughts, and behavior from the people around them before they have language to explain it. Infants develop their ideas about who they are by how they are treated. If responded to with delight and caring, they learn that they are delightful and important. If not adequately responded to, or abused, they learn that they are bad and not worth caring for and have no allies. Kids develop their sense of cultural, ethnic, gender, and personal identities by experiencing the thousands of cultural messages in the media, their schools, their neighborhoods, and their families. As a therapist, you will not want to mess with the positive introjects, like "I'm a lovable, capable person, who can achieve anything I want to." You will definitely want to go after those with the message that "I'm not enough. People like me are stupid. Because of who I am, there's no chance for me." When you identify these familial, social, and cultural introjects as solid objects, you can help your clients pull them out, throw them away, and replace them with true, current, and chosen beliefs and feeling states. They are rarely full-blown ego states, but they are malleable states that are very useful to transform. This intervention has pieces from narrative (White & Epston, 1990), hypnotic, and neurolinguistic programming (Bandler & Grinder, 1975) therapies.

Cultural expectations may be clearly negative: "working-class people are stupid," "Blacks are criminals," "Indians are lazy," "blondes are ditzy." Positive expectations may also have negative effects: "women should be slender and cute," "big boys never cry," "Asians or Jews should be brilliant," "good people are employed and need no help from anyone." Failure to fit cultural expectations can be nearly as oppressive as living in a victimized group. Of course, one person may be subject to both negative and positive cultural beliefs.

When I think about internalized oppression, I borrow the idea of introjects from object relations theory (Klein, 1968/2001), in which introjects are defined as psychic objects that are unconsciously taken in by a person. These "objects" may be emotional states, ideas, or even an ego state of another person or group (Ogden, 1991). Michael White's (1995) narrative therapy describes personal, familial, organizational, and cultural/historical narratives from which people create their reality and sense of self. In narrative therapy, problems are externalized, disowned, and conquered. Generational and cultural traumas, narratives, and ego states can be externalized and consciously disowned. I found that by using narrative questions, introjects, and the two-hand technique, I was able to create quick and relatively painless ways to move entrenched cultural distress (Shapiro, 2005b).

Steps to clear introjects

1. Identify the belief and how it got into the client. *What are you saying about yourself? How did that belief get into you?*

2. Identify where and what it is inside the body: *What sensation goes with that? What emotion goes with that? Where does that feeling live? Is it a solid object or a substance? What shape is it? What substance is it? What color is it?*

3. Get your client's agreement that she doesn't want it anymore: *Is that something you want to have inside of you?* (Ninety-nine percent of the time clients say "No!" One percent of the time you need to ask more questions: *How is it serving you?* Or, *What part of you is afraid of letting that go?*)

4. Have the client move his arms and imaginally grab handfuls of the stuff, pull it out, and throw it away. Keep going until it's all gone. This could take up to five minutes or be done in less than thirty seconds. *Imagine a hatch has opened in the floor between us. Now bring your hands to that gunk in your belly, pull that stuff out, and throw it down the hatch. That's right, keep pulling! . . . What percent is gone? Great! Keep pulling until it's all out of there. It's all gone now? Great! Let's flush that stuff now and shut that hatch door.* (Believe it or not, most clients can and will do this.)

5. Replace the contents of that place with positive, chosen states, colors, and sensations: *What would you like there instead? What about acceptance? What sensation goes with that? What emotion? What color is it? Is it a texture or a solid object?*

6. Send the new, chosen state through the entire body: *Are you ready to bring that state of love and acceptance to your whole body? Breathe into it and breathe it through every cell. Breathe it into your whole torso, your shoulders and arms, your neck and*

head, your pelvis, your legs, and all the way to your toes. Notice
if any part of you needs an extra dose. Send it there.

7.   Assign the client homework: noticing the change outside
     the therapy office

If you are an EMDR therapist, use bilateral stimulation with
steps 4 and 6.

Kinds of introjects

III   Goodness and badness, usually relative to how the client
      was treated
III   Sufficiency, a sense of being "enough" for a situation or
      person
III   Acceptability
III   Appearance
III   Class
III   Ethnicity
III   Disability/ability
III   Intelligence
III   Success/achievement
III   Safety
III   Emotions, especially fear, anger, and shame
III   Gender expectations
   I   Presentation (masculinity/femininity)
   I   Sexual orientation
   I   Gender syntonic (the majority) or transgender

CASE EXAMPLE **Parentectomy**

Wanda was an unwanted child. She had an older sister, and her parents had reconciled themselves to loving the unplanned baby, if it was a boy. She had more than once heard her parents arguing about her birth, blaming themselves for her existence. Wanda was often ignored and casually physically abused: slapped when she walked into a room. She spent much of her life hunkered down, trying to become "good enough" through good grades, good deeds, and being quiet, rarely asking for what she needed. She came to me in her mid-thirties, depressed, resentful, and feeling failure despite her advanced degree and high-level job in a wonderful nonprofit. We did trauma work, including EMDR and ego state work about the abuse, the neglect, and the last narcissistic boyfriend. We connected her grown-up nurturer with her child parts and did some great therapy. Some of the depression lifted, but the negative self-talk and her refusal to ever put own needs into any social equation persisted. Finally, we performed a parentectomy and things changed.

> *Wanda, I want you to think of all the ways that your parents told you that you didn't matter: the things they said, they things they did, and the things they didn't do . . . Where are you holding all of that in your body?*
> My chest and my neck.
>
> *What's the sensation in those places?*
> Heavy and kind of like nausea.
>
> *What kind of emotion goes with that?*

Defeated and sad and sort of hopeless.

Is that like a solid object or is it more diffuse?
It's not an object. It's like gunk that fills everything.

What color is that gunk?
Dark gray.

What texture is it?
It's like a thick paste.

Do you want to keep it or get rid of it?
Get rid of it! It's time to get rid of it!

*I agree! So put on your thick gardening gloves. You don't want
to touch this stuff—it's toxic! And see the hole in the floor that
opened up between us? You got it? . . . Now grab as much as you
can and throw it down the hole. Keep going until it's completely
gone . . . What percent is left?*
Twenty-five.

Keep going.
(After another few minutes, she slows down.) *Is it all out of you?
Great! I'll slam the lid on the floor hatch. You stomp on the floor lever
to flush it to the center of the earth. Good. What do you notice now?*
(Excitedly) I feel lighter and taller.

*Great! Enjoy that for a moment . . . Now would you like to choose
what you want in those places instead?*
Of course! I want to feel like I'm okay.

Self-acceptance and self-love?
Yes.

What color goes with love and acceptance?
A deep pink.

What texture is that?
Foamy, like a stiff whipped cream.

Bring that deep pink foamy love and acceptance into your neck, your shoulders, and your chest. Fill them completely up. Fill all the nooks and crannies.
(Wanda smiles, looking dreamy.) That's good stuff!

What's it feel like to have that pink foamy love and acceptance in those places?
It's new and good and like it should be.

Let's expand it through your whole body.
Okay!

Breathe that pink foamy love and acceptance through your whole body, your whole torso, up through your neck to your head. Saturate your brain, your face, your hair, and the rest of your head with it. Bring it through your shoulders, through your arms all the way to the ends of your fingers. Bring it through your torso down to your pelvis, your butt, and down through your legs. Bring extra to any parts of your body that you haven't accepted or that's brought you pain. Make sure you get your bones, all your organs, and your entire blood stream . . . What do you notice now?

It's good . . . I know I'm good.

Let's think about how to keep this going all week. How many times a day do want to notice this love and acceptance stuff?
Several.

You've got a smartphone. Do you want to set alarms for remembering? How many times?
I have a natural break between clients once an hour. I can set it for then, depending on my schedule. I'll set it for the rest of today, and then set it each day.

Could anything occur that could bring back some gunk?
Talking to my mom could do that. What do I do then?

Pull out whatever gunk you get from your mom, or anyone, flush it again, and bring in the pink. You can do that all by yourself.
I definitely will.

In the next session, Wanda appeared lighter and happier. She reported that she was recognizing the positive people around her at work, people she had been anxious around before. She was speaking up more in meetings and was becoming more assertive. During her weekly call to her mother, she did absorb some "gunk" but immediately pulled it out. In the next weeks, she found herself being less "absorbent" of her mother's disregard of her during mom's self-absorbed monologs.

CASE EXAMPLES Cultural Introjects

Here are some brief examples of clearing several common culture introjects: body image, money, masculinity/bullying, and parental and cultural expectations.

BODY IMAGE

The two-hand technique can be useful to address body image introjects.

> *Hold the body you think you should have in one hand, and that middle-age body you have in the other. What do you notice? How did those ideas about bodies get into you? Where do they live inside you? What are they made of? What color, what texture . . . ? Does your oldest, wisest self want to keep those cultural ideas about what a person should look like? Are you ready to pull them out of you? . . . What do you want there instead? . . . Bring it in . . . Imagine looking in the mirror, at your middle-age body, through your own eyes. What do you see now? What do you feel now?*

People often have a grief response, which is different from the shame they were living under. Let them grieve the body they don't have on the way to accepting the body they have now.

MONEY

George is a middle-aged black man from a poor family, who has a successful job, a great relationship with a good man, and a strong social network. One of his many anxieties involved the sense of not having enough money to survive.

Your great grandparents were sharecroppers. Your grandparents and parents had barely enough to get by. You make ten times your father's salary, and you're afraid to spend any of it. Think of all the ways your family let you know that there wasn't enough. Remember how they scrimped and saved. Now think of your 401(k), your savings account, and what the financial planner told you that you could afford to live on. In one hand, hold the family messages. In the other, the money you have and the money you earn. Visualize the numbers . . . Do you need your family's fears in order to make reasonable decisions about money? No? Then let's go get them. Feel the place where that fear lives. What's it feel like? Is it a solid object or a substance? What's it made of? What color? How big is it? Are you ready to pull it out? . . . What goes there instead? That good sense that you already have? Great! What does that feel like? Look like? What's it made of? Spread it through your whole body . . . Now imagine yourself using that money, guided by your good sense, to take care of yourself.

MASCULINITY / BULLYING

Teenagers are obsessed with social norms and are often shamed or assaulted for not fitting into them. Many kids are bullied for not fitting into rigid gender norms. Since most kids buy into those arbitrary definitions, it's helpful to separate who they are from who society says they should be, affirm them, and give them some tools to deal with the harassment.

So you're fourteen, you hate sports, you love art, and you've got a sensitive nature. So when people hassle you, it really hurts. You're getting bullied at school, and you hate yourself. Who do those ass-holes at school think you're supposed to be?

I'm supposed to be bigger, more macho and athletic, not into art.

Think about being that guy. What do you think of him?
I don't like him. I wouldn't hang out with someone like that.

Who would you hang out with?
I'd be with people who are nice to people and let them be who they are. And I'd be with other people into drawing, and comic books, that sort of thing.

Do you know any of those people?
Yes. I've got some friends online, and a few people at school.

Do they think you're okay?
Yeah, pretty much.

I want you to find that place in you that holds the picture of what those bullies think you should be . . . Is that you? No? Could you pull that picture out of you, since it's not you? Take the photo by the edge and pull it out. Now flip it back at those guys. You might say, "This is yours, not mine and not me."
Done.

What could you put inside that place, instead?
I'm putting a drawing of mine that I really like.

What feeling goes with that drawing?
Like pride and a sense of doing well. I got lots of likes when I posted that picture on Facebook, and it felt good. I liked it before I posted it.

Can you let that proud feeling spread through your whole body?
Breathe it through. Stick in your bloodstream, and let it course
through everywhere.
This is cool.

Sort of like you, right now. Hang with it for a while . . . I want
you to imagine getting hassled by those jerks, and bringing up this
feeling. What do you do?
I just walk by . . . It's not about me.

That is so cool!

PARENTAL AND CULTURAL EXPECTATIONS

"Positive" expectations of ethnicity, gender, and social class can
be heavy burdens. Here's an example of disowning a heavy "positive" expectation.

So if you were the perfect Chinese daughter, who would you be?
I'd be more academic. I'd be more ambitious. And I'd have
another body, not be as boxy-shaped.

Explain the ambitious part to me. I see you as very goal oriented.
I want what I want, but they're the wrong things. I'm working
for the environment, in a low-level job, in a low-level agency.
I should be a high-level executive somewhere, making money
and marrying a real go-getter.

What do you feel, when you think about that woman you're sup-
posed to be?
With you, I feel okay. If I think about being with my family

or my parent's friends, I feel bad, like I'm not measuring up, like I'm the flaky one.

Where do you feel that inside?
It's in my chest and the pit of my stomach.

What's that feel like?
It feels tight and kind of nauseating. I think I'm ashamed.

Is there a color and shape to that shame?
It's dark and like a burr—prickly everywhere.

Is that something you want to have around?
No!

Great! Could you call up that rich, high-powered executive you're supposed to be, you know, the one with the trophy husband? (She nods.) *What would you like to tell her about yourself and your worth?*
I'm trying to save her world from extinction, by slowing down climate change. It's a worthwhile thing, and it fits me and my values. I'm never going to be her. I don't want to be, even if I feel bad about it sometimes.

Do you need her around to remind you of who you're not?
No, she pretends to be "good" without being real.

Could you reach inside and pull her out and the dark, prickly shame out? (Five minutes pass while she pulls and makes a ball in her hands.) *And can you send both of them back to your*

parents' house? When she gets there, I wonder if she'll melt back into your parents.
She did!

What's that like?
I feel like I'm different: taller and lighter.

Breathe that through you. Take it everywhere inside.
She was the good kid who did everything right but wasn't really me. I mean, I'm doing the right things for me and for the planet, but not for them or that whole community in Vancouver. Or at least they don't think so.

Imagine going home to visit without carrying the daughter that you didn't turn out to be with you.
Well, she already lives there with them. But, you know, they love me anyway, and they want me to be successful so that I'll survive. I think I'm surviving just fine. I need to remember that when I'm there. And my parents and my sibs have enough money that they don't need my help that way. I'll be the one that goes back there when someone gets sick, not the successful ones.

You're not successful?
I am. I'm a successful me. And I'm not going to starve or need their support, which is one of their fears, not mine.

ABUSECTOMIES

People who experienced constant abuse often "carry" the instruments of that abuse inside. These survivors are often high on the dissociative spectrum and "split" their perpetrators as well as themselves. Whether it is the fists, body parts, voices, or belts of the perpetrators, the representations can get lodged into clients, and we can help facilitate their removal. Many trauma therapies, especially EMDR and somatic therapies, can successfully dislodge the sensations and feeling of the objects. When these or other therapies are not adequate, try this direct approach.

CASE EXAMPLE **Dickectomy**

Betsy had been sexually abused by many men in a cult situation when she was five years old. She was a polyfragmented DID client, who had done six years of intensive psychotherapy and still had a long way (about twelve more years) to go. We had worked on her vaginal and oral rapes, and all her parts knew that she had survived them. Parts of her still carried constant sensations of penises. We used a dissociative table technique (Fraser, 2003), which we had used many times before, to find her appropriate ego states/dissociative parts and then went to work.

Betsy, can you go inside, find all the parts that still feel a dick in their throats or a dick in their vaginas, and bring them to the Meeting Place?
Give me a minute . . . Okay, we're all here.

How many of you?

Four, that I know of.

All kids?
All kids from three years old to almost five.

What kind of kids?
(She sighs.) One angry, one limp and giving up, and one scared, and one watching from the ceiling. (The usual crew of parts that split during abuse.)

Let's orient all parts to right now. You know how to do this. Let's start here. Let those kid parts look through your eyes and see this office and me. Tell them who I am and who you are, and have them notice that those cult guys aren't around. Have them notice how tall you are right now, about three feet taller than a five-year-old. What would do if anybody tried to mess with you now?
If that person survived what I'd do to them, I'd call the cops (aggressively).

Now show those little ones the rest of your life, where you live now . . . your job and the people there . . . your friends . . . and your dog. Are there any cult people in your current life? Show them how safe it is. . . . Take a poll, and ask these kids if they want to get rid of the dicks.
They want to, but they don't believe that they can.

What do you (the grown-up/ANP) think?
I'm tired of choking, and we've done weirder things, so why not this?

That's the spirit! Let's go! All parts involved will have to do this

*at the same time, even if it's a little different for different parts.
Are y'all ready?*
Everyone's ready.

*First some stupid therapy questions: Are any parts of you currently
being raped?*
No, we're not.

Are there real penises inside of you?
No. Even the little ones know that, even if it feels like there is.

*Good! Start with the vaginas. Can y'all feel the sensation of being
a little girl with an adult penis inside?*
Yeah, we all feel them in there (in a low tone).

Is it like a normal penis, or different?
Different for different people: one is like on fire, one is like a
knife, the other ones are like real ones, but big and moving
around.

*Can you tell everyone to put appropriate gloves on: an oven mitt
for the hot one, gardening gloves for the sharp one, surgical gloves
for the regular ones?*
I told them, and they're doing it.

When you pull the penises out, how are y'all disposing of them?
We are throwing them in the nuclear incinerator.

*Okay, gloves on! Grab the back end of those things. Since they're solid,
one big pull should do it. If it takes more, do more. One, two, three, go!*

(She yanks her arms up from her pelvis and pitches the imaginary penis. A minute passes.) They're all burned up, and something is weird.

What happened?
There is only one little girl left.

I think I know what happened. Do you know?
Their jobs were holding that one yucky feeling, and with the feeling gone, they integrated, like we did before.

I think so, too. Let's finish this, and then discuss it.
Okay.

What do you want to be feeling down there instead?
Safety and just me.

Does safety have a color?
Blue.

Feel just you and the sensations of just you with nothing else going on. Surround your whole pelvis, vagina, and womb with blue safety, inside and out.

In the next session, we did the oral rapes and pulled the penises out of three little girls, one who was asphyxiated and limp, one who was fighting, and one who was scared. These kids also integrated together when the penises were thrown in the incinerator. Later that day, I got a phone call from Betsy.

You're never going to believe what happened! I had dinner!

Can you explain to me why that is so exciting?
Because I don't think I've actually experienced the sensations and tastes of eating since I was five years old. I felt the food in my mouth and I tasted it. I ate really slowly and I didn't eat too much, like I usually do. Wow!

Wow is right!

Over the weeks, Betsy reported that her eating habits had changed. She no longer binged, was more selective in her diet, and was having more fun eating. She lost about thirty extra pounds, settling to a good and solid, but no longer heavy weight.

INTROJECTS: WRAPPING UP

Whether introjects are critical parents, unattainable ideals, ethnic or cultural stereotypes, or objects of abuse, they can be identified, pulled out, and thrown out. When working with dissociative clients, make sure you don't pull out and throw out any parts of the self. Parts can be transformed, temporarily confined to safe or holding places, or integrated, but not tossed.

REFERENCES

Aron, E. (1996). *The highly sensitive person*. New York, NY: Broadway Books.

Azevedo, F. A., Carvalho, L. R., Grinberg, L. T., Farfel, J. M., Ferretti, R. E., Leite, R. E., . . . Herculano-Houzel, S. (2009). Equal numbers of neuronal and nonneuronal cells make the human brain an isometrically scaled-up primate brain. *Journal of Comparative Neurology, 513*(5), 532–541. http://dx.doi.org/10.1002/cne.21974.

Bader, E., & Pearson, P. (1988). *In quest of the mythical mate*. New York, NY: Brunner/Mazel.

Bandler, R., & Grinder, J. (1975). *The structure of magic*, Vol. 1: *A book about language and therapy*. Palo Alto, CA: Science and Behavior Books.

Berne, E. (1964). *Games people play*. New York, NY: Grove Press.

Bernstein, E. M., & Putnam, F. W. (1986). Development, reliability, and validity of a dissociation scale. *Journal of Nervous and Mental Disease, 174*, 727–735.

Bowlby, J. (1969), *Attachment and loss*, Vol. 1: *Attachment*. New York, NY: Basic Books.

Bowlby, J. (1973). *Attachment and loss*, Vol. 2: *Separation*. New York, NY: Basic Books.

Cozolino, L. (2006). *The neuroscience of human relationship: Attachment and the developing social brain*. New York, NY: Norton.

Fosha, D. (2000). *The transforming power of affect: A model for accelerated change*. New York, NY: Basic Books.

Fraser, G. A. (2003). Fraser's dissociative table technique revisited, revised: A strategy for working with ego states in dissociative disorders and ego state therapy. *Dissociation, 44*, 5–28.

Freud, S. (1933, 1962). *New introductory lectures on psychoanalysis*. New York, NY: Penguin.

Gilligan, S. (1996). Lecture at Training Group, Leavenworth, Washington.

Gottman, J. M., & Silver, N. (1999). The two kinds of marital conflict. Chapter 7 in *The Seven Principles for Making Marriages Work* (pp. 129–155). New York, NY: Three Rivers Press.

Grand, D. (2013). *Brainspotting: The revolutionary new therapy for rapid and effective change*. Boulder, CO: Sounds True.

Haley, J. (1973). *Uncommon therapy: The psychiatric techniques of Milton H. Erickson, M.D.* New York, NY: Norton.

Hughes, D., & Baylin, J. (2012). *Brain-based parenting: The neuroscience of caregiving for healthy attachment*. New York, NY: Norton.

Kernberg, O.F. (1993). Convergences and divergences in contemporary psychoac. technique., *Int. J. Psychoanal.*, 74:659-674

Kiessling, R. (2005). Integrating resource development strategies into your EMDR practice. *EMDR solutions: Pathways to healing* (pp. 57–87) New York, NY. Norton.

Kitchur, M. (2005). The strategic developmental model for EMDR. *EMDR Solutions: Pathways to healing.* (pp. 8–56) New York, NY. Norton.

Klein, M. (2001). *Envy and gratitude.* Cambridge, UK: Tavistock. (Original work published 1968)

Knipe, J. (2005). Targeting positive affect to clear the pain of unrequited love, codependence, avoidance, and procrastination. In R. Shapiro (Ed.), *EMDR solutions: Pathways to healing* (pp.189–207) New York, NY: Norton.

Knipe, J. (2014). *EMDR toolbox: Theory and treatment of complex PTSD and dissociation.* New York, NY: Springer.

Kohut, H. (1971). *The analysis of the self.* Chicago, Il. University of Chicago Press.

Korn, D. L., & Leeds, A. M. (2002). Preliminary evidence of efficacy for EMDR resource development and installation in the stabilization phase of treatment of complex posttraumatic stress disorder. *Journal of Clinical Psychology, 58*(12), 1465–1487.

Leeds, A. (2009). *A guide to the standard EMDR protocols for clinicians, supervisors, and consultants.* New York, NY: Springer.

Manfield, P. (1992). *Split self/split object: Understanding and treating borderline, narcissistic and schizoid disorders.* Lanham, MD. Rowman & Littlefield.

Masterson, J.F. (1981). *The narcissistic and borderline disorders: An integrated developmental approach.* New York, NY. Brunner-Routledge.

Miller, A. (1981). *The drama of the gifted child.* New York, NY: Basic Books.

National Institute of Mental Health. (2009). Suicide in the U.S.: Statistics and prevention. NIH Publication No. 06–45. Retrieved July 31, 2014, from http://www.lb7.uscourts.gov/documents/08-42261.pdf.

Ogden, P. (2006). *Trauma and the body: A sensorimotor approach to psychotherapy.* New York, NY. Norton.

Pace, P. (2007). *Lifespan integration: Connecting ego-states through time.* Retrieved 7/5/2014 from http://www.lifespanintegration .com/book.php.

Panksepp, J. (1998). *Affective neuroscience: The foundations of human and animal emotions.* New York, NY: Oxford University Press.

Parnell, L. (2013). *Attachment-focused EMDR: Healing relational trauma.* New York, NY: Norton.

Porges, S. W. (2011). *The polyvagal theory: Neurophysiological foundations of emotions, attachment, communication, and self-regulation.* New York, NY: Norton.

Putnam, F. (1997). *Dissociation in children and adolescents.* New York, NY: Guilford Press.

Ross, C. A. (1997). *Dissociative identity disorder: Diagnosis, clinical features, and treatment of multiple personality* (2nd ed.). New York, NY: Wiley.

Schmidt, S. J. (2009). *The developmental needs meeting strategy: A model for healing adults with childhood attachment wounds.* San Antonio, TX: DNMS Institute.

Schnarch, D. (1997). *Passionate marriage.* New York, NY: Norton.

Schore, A. N. (1994). *Affect regulation and the origin of the self: The neurobiology of emotional development.* Hillsdale, NJ: Erlbaum.

Schwartz, R. (1995). *Internal family systems therapy.* New York, NY: Guilford Press.

Shapiro, F. (2001). *Eye movement desensitization and reprocessing: Basic principles, protocols and procedures* (2nd ed.). New York, NY: Guilford Press.

Shapiro, R. (2005a). Cultural and generational introjects. In R. Shapiro (Ed.), *EMDR solutions: Pathways to healing.* pp. 228–240. New York, NY: Norton.

Shapiro, R. (2005b). The two-hand interweave. In R. Shapiro (Ed.), *EMDR solutions: Pathways to healing* pp.161–166. New York, NY: Norton.

Shapiro, R. (2010). *Trauma treatment handbook: Protocols across the spectrum.* New York, NY: Norton.

Sheldon, B. W., & Sheldon, A. (2010) Complex integration of multiple brain systems. Retrieved 7/10/2015 from http://www.complexintegrationmbs.com/?page-id=62

Siegel, D. J. (1999). *The developing mind: Toward a neurobiology of interpersonal experience.* New York, NY: Guilford Press.

Steele, A. (2007a). *Developing a secure self: An attachment-based approach to adult psychotherapy* (2nd ed.). Retrieved Month Day, Year, from http://www.april-steele.ca/

Steele, A. (2007b). *Developing a secure self handbook.* Retrieved Month Day, Year, from http://www.april-steele.ca/handbook-toolkit.php

Tronick, E., Adamson, L. B., Als, H., & Brazelton, T. B. (1975, April). Infant emotions in normal and pertubated interactions. Paper presented at the biennial meeting of the Society for Research in Child Development, Denver, CO.

Tronick, E. Still Face Experiment: Retrieved from www.youtube.com/watch?v=apzXGEbZht0 7/10/2014.

Twombly, J. (2005). EMDR for clients with DID, DDNOS, and ego states. In R. Shapiro (Ed.), *EMDR solutions: Pathways to healing* (pp. 88–120). New York, NY: Norton.

Twombly, J., & Schwartz, R. (2008). The integration of the internal family systems model (IFS) and EMDR. In C. Forgash

& M. Copeley (Eds.), *Healing the heart of trauma and dissoci-ation.* (pp. 295–312.) New York, NY: Springer.

van der Hart, O., Nijenhuis, E., & Steele, K. (2006). *The haunted self: Structural dissociation and the treatment of chronic trauma-tization.* New York, NY: Norton.

Watkins, H., & Watkins, J. (1997). *Ego states: Theory and therapy.* New York, NY: Norton.

White, M., & Epston, D. (1995). *Narrative means to therapeutic ends.* New York, NY: Norton.

INDEX